THE EXTRAORDINARY POWER OF LEADER HUMILITY

THE
EXTRAORDINARY
POWER OF
LEADER
HUMILITY

Thriving Organizations—Great Results

MARILYN GIST, PHD

Foreword and Guest Chapter by

ALAN MULALLY

Former CEO of Ford Motor Company
and Boeing Commercial Airplanes

Berrett-Koehler Publishers, Inc.

Berrett-Koehler Publishers, Inc.
1333 Broadway, Suite 1000
Oakland, CA 94612-1921
Tel: (510) 817-2277
Fax: (510) 817-2278
www.bkconnection.com

ORDERING INFORMATION
Quantity sales. Special discounts are available on quantity purchases by corporations, associations, and others. For details, contact the "Special Sales Department" at the Berrett-Koehler address above.
Individual sales. Berrett-Koehler publications are available through most bookstores. They can also be ordered directly from Berrett-Koehler: Tel: (800) 929-2929; Fax: (802) 864-7626; www.bkconnection.com.
Orders for college textbook/course adoption use. Please contact Berrett-Koehler: Tel: (800) 929-2929; Fax: (802) 864-7626.

Distributed to the U.S. trade and internationally by Penguin Random House Publisher Services.

Berrett-Koehler and the BK logo are registered trademarks of Berrett-Koehler Publishers, Inc.

Printed in Canada

Berrett-Koehler books are printed on long-lasting acid-free paper. When it is available, we choose paper that has been manufactured by environmentally responsible processes. These may include using trees grown in sustainable forests, incorporating recycled paper, minimizing chlorine in bleaching, or recycling the energy produced at the paper mill.

Library of Congress Cataloging-in-Publication Data
Name: Gist, Marilyn Elaine, author.
Title: The extraordinary power of leader humility : thriving organizations — great results / Marilyn Gist, PhD ; with foreword and guest chapter by Alan Mulally, former CEO of Ford Motor Company and Boeing Commercial Airlines.
Description: 1st Edition. | Oakland : Berrett-Koehler Publishers, 2020. | Includes bibliographical references and index.
Identifiers: LCCN 2020011383 | ISBN 9781523089666 (hardcover) | ISBN 9781523089673 (pdf) | ISBN 9781523089680 (epub)
Subjects: LCSH: Leadership. | Communication in management. | Humility.
Classification: LCC HD57.7 .G564 2020 | DDC 658.4/092—dc23
LC record available at https://lccn.loc.gov/2020011383

First Edition
26 25 24 23 22 21 20   10 9 8 7 6 5 4 3 2 1

Book producer: Linda Jupiter Productions; *Proofreader:* Mary Kanable
Copyeditor: Elissa Rabellino; *Indexer:* Paula C. Durbin-Westby
Text designer/illustrator: Kim Scott, Bumpy Design; *Cover designer:* Adam Johnson

*To leaders everywhere who care to serve the greater good
and support the dignity of all stakeholders*

*In honor of family, friends,
and the Source of all Life*

Contents

Foreword

While CEO of Ford Motor Company and Boeing Commercial Airplanes, I had the honor to lead the work of hundreds of thousands of people and coordinate with our many stakeholders. I know firsthand how important it is for leaders to have humility. And it is going to be even more important for leaders of the future—and for our society of the future. That's because, more than ever before, we need to be able to work together worldwide to maintain our quality of life and to resolve big, important global and local issues. Humility, especially leader humility, is the foundation for working together in a healthy and high-performance way.

Yet, in my experience, leader humility is relatively uncommon. I have often seen leaders who have more humility than what they exhibit when actually leading. I think this is part of the leadership model still very alive today where we assume the leader is supposed to know all and use command and control. That is also the leadership model still embraced by many stakeholders: investors, suppliers, government, and so on. I believe this will only change when all the stakeholders move toward a new model for the leader of the future—one of being a facilitator and coach, leading with humility, love, and service. This change in the leadership model will come only when we see more examples of it delivering better value for all the stakeholders and the greater good. So, this book will really help because it shows a better way to lead and provides powerful examples that can be widely understood.

Leadership humility enhances and enables inclusion, participation, commitment, innovation, safety, excitement, discipline, caring, adaptability, and continuous improvement—to name just a few of its positive outcomes! It is at the heart of the operating process and Expected Behaviors in my Working Together Management System™, which creates a smart and safe organization and one that increases quality, productivity, and performance, while reducing costs, for the benefit of all stakeholders and the greater good.

For the past five years, Marilyn Gist has been a colleague, friend, and kindred spirit because of *who* she is, *what* she does, and *how* she does it. She has a long and distinguished record of successful service in the formation and development of other leaders. I might add that I did extensive research before deciding whom I believed in and wanted to work with. Marilyn did the same, and we selected each other. We came to understand early on that we are very aligned in our desire to serve and further contribute to developing leaders.

I have gotten to know her through our work, which has involved teaching, writing, and many conversations on the important responsibilities of leadership: compelling visions, comprehensive strategies for achieving them, and relentless implementation. We also agree that who you are is going to have the most important contribution to your leadership success. The main elements of this are your authenticity, humility, love, and service. Marilyn's character and competencies are wonderful and inspirational. Our working together has produced some great results for leadership formation and development of students, faculty, and publications on Working Together and leadership.

Marilyn is exceptionally qualified to write this book. In addition to her extensive, most successful career in educating others around leadership, her own personal and leadership humility inform her understanding of the subject. Readers will benefit because, of all the things Marilyn could share and teach us, the power of humility is at the top of the list. And it is humility in general, and the extended power of leadership humility, that enable everything required for us all to work together for the greater good, enjoy each other, and have fun.

I truly like this book! It is focused, comprehensive, and compelling. It's easy to read and most understandable. Our world needs humble leaders more than ever to help us deal with issues that are so big, important, pressing, and personal. Only by working together are we going to not only save our world, but create a world based on respect for human dignity, and inclusion and growth for all of us.

Marilyn's definition of leadership humility is simple and clear: "Leader humility is a tendency to feel and display a deep regard for others' dignity." It is a way to be. It is a way to live. It is right. It is useful. It enables everything. The book does a great job of showing us what humility really is—and what it is not. It is certainly not weakness or meekness. Genuine humility is a sign of confidence and strength. The model advanced in this book is terrific because it is based on the three questions we all have about those who lead and shows the six keys to demonstrating humility, so that we support others' dignity. The model is comprehensive and actionable. I believe that when leaders read this, they will be compelled to try the keys described. Then they will see positive results and further develop their leadership humility. This will generate continuous leadership improvement, effectiveness, and happiness—for the leader and all of the stakeholders. We need and want the hearts and minds of everyone to move forward together.

In addition to the model of leader humility, part of what makes this book so valuable are the experiences, observations, and advice offered from the CEOs that Marilyn interviewed. These are great and successful leaders of great organizations. The leaders are diverse and inspirational, and they lead with humility. They are very special leaders who focus on the greater good.

Marilyn has captured a vital enabling element of the leader of the future—humility! This book explains just why this is so important. Equally important, it shows us how to do it. Appreciating and improving leader humility is a great opportunity to enhance our leadership service. It is essential so that we can engage everyone's hearts and minds and work together to move us forward positively in our rapidly changing world.

Alan Mulally
Former president and CEO, Ford Motor Company;
former president and CEO, Boeing Commercial Airplanes;
former president, Boeing Information, Space and Defense Systems

Preface

Seattle has spawned many organizations with global impact whose success and innovation have changed the way we live and work. The city thrives on energies from Amazon, Boeing, Costco, Microsoft, Starbucks, and the Bill & Melinda Gates Foundation, to name only a few. It is in this rich climate that I have been fortunate to lead business executive programs at two universities for the past two decades. This gave me the opportunity to work with a number of CEOs who are brilliant leaders. I have been inspired by their commitment to leading well and privileged to see the positive effects they have on followers and organizational outcomes. I have also seen the negative effects caused by many other leaders—and I have made and learned from mistakes of my own.

Over time, it became clear to me that there is one variable at the heart of leadership that is far too often overlooked. That variable is *humility*. It guides a leader's behaviors by placing central importance on the fact that *others' dignity* matters. This book shines a light on this underrecognized subject. It explains why leader humility is so needed—and it shows how leaders can improve performance by knowing and using the six keys to leader humility that others monitor very closely. This is not merely my opinion. There is sound research on the value of humility in leadership. And there are great leaders who prove that humility works.

It is timely and urgent that we talk about this topic. Events on our world stage highlight issues of character and behavior among leaders as they grapple with very complex problems. In the United States and abroad, many people are appalled by the arrogance and lack of integrity we see at the highest levels of *government*. Nearly all feel dismayed by our leaders' collective dysfunction as we face global challenges like a viral pandemic, trade, immigration, climate change, and information accuracy. Most people want a better approach to leadership.

The need for better *business* leadership is equally urgent. Businesses face many complex challenges: volatile economies, technological change, global markets for trade and labor, cybersecurity, impacts of climate change, and a younger generation that is jaded from past corporate misdeeds and adept at using social media to expose missteps. Business executives need to engage well with employees, customers, shareholders, community activists, and regulators who often have strong and conflicting views. In order to succeed, leaders must be able to bring divergent groups together and forge consensus on a path forward. Power plays, personal attacks, and harsh elbows work entirely against this. And without leadership that can align these stakeholders, businesses can't generate profits, sustain growth, support diversity, innovate, or contribute positively to the needs of society.

Fundamentally, leadership requires *working together*. We need leaders who can do this well to resolve our global and domestic challenges, whether in business, nonprofits, or government. And leader humility—a tendency to feel and display deep regard for others' dignity—is essential for working together well with all stakeholders.

It is now so important for us to understand the imperative of leader humility for working together that I was moved to write this book to show its extraordinary power as a way forward. As part of this project, I interviewed a select group of twelve prominent presidents and CEOs of major organizations who embrace a humble approach to leadership. My sample is small, yet compelling: these leaders represent dynamic companies, most of which are global in scope with widely recognized brand names. Collectively, these leaders employ hundreds of thousands of people, manage or generate trillions of dollars of revenue each year, and contribute significantly to domestic and/or global productivity. The richness of the book is that it draws not only on my experience but on the collective wisdom of these highly successful leaders. The book also discusses how leader humility applies to large organizations as well as to smaller ones.

If you want to lead well, this book is designed for you. The material here is appropriate for current leaders of all levels across industry, government, and nonprofit organizations. It is also appropriate for aspiring leaders, as well as for graduate students of business, educational administration, and public affairs. If you work in leadership development, this book holds content that is important for change agents and organizational leaders who select and develop leaders. And if you are another type of stakeholder, such as someone who works for leaders or chooses leaders by voting, this book should help you by sharpening your understanding of effective versus ineffective leader behaviors.

Chapters 1 through 3 provide an essential foundation for understanding leader humility. They show why it is important for working together by linking it to human dignity. They include a model of leader humility that is derived from three questions people ask or wonder about leaders and the behaviors that people monitor when forming their own answers. Chapters 4 through 6 take the three questions one at a time, explaining specific behaviors (keys) that demonstrate leader humility. These chapters tie behaviors that are under a leader's control to leadership responsibilities—such as attracting and retaining talent, diversity management, and so on— and provide a list of dos and don'ts. Ideas for action are included in most chapters throughout the book.

The third section of the book brings the material together and shows how it is integrated in practice. Chapter 7 is guest-authored by Alan Mulally, who explains his well-regarded Working Together Management System and shows how it is anchored in humility. Chapter 8 illustrates how these ideas scale to smaller organizations and how leader humility generates thriving versus toxic organizations. It also provides examples of organizational policies that support others' dignity. Chapter 9 offers my observations on factors that led to humility formation across the CEOs I interviewed, suggests how it can be developed in adult leaders, and provides reflection, questions, and exercises for developing personal humility. Bios of each of the leaders I interviewed are included here. In chapter 10, the book closes by discussing the relevance of this material for business and beyond.

In my experience, most leaders—and aspiring leaders—want to be highly effective. This book holds essential information to help you do that, because leader humility is subtle yet very powerful for working together. It is the secret that many leaders need to create thriving organizations and great results.

Marilyn Gist
Seattle, Washington

THE EXTRAORDINARY POWER OF LEADER HUMILITY

CHAPTER ONE

Leading as Relationship

Leadership is about inspiring people to do what's needed. If you look over your shoulder and no one's following you, you are not a leader.

—Roger Ferguson, president and CEO, TIAA

Leadership requires *working together*. Being in relationship and working with others is how we make progress. And a leader's biggest challenge is to inspire in others their enthusiastic engagement with a shared goal, whether that is to launch a new product, advance an important cause, improve financial performance, or resolve global challenges.

So how can leaders work most effectively with others? When we think about factors that drive organizational performance, we tend to think about innovation, capital, and strong competitive strategy. When we talk about motivating people, conversation typically turns to rewards and compensation. Largely unnoticed is leader humility—an extraordinarily powerful way of influencing those around you to volunteer their full support to achieving shared goals. Collins (2001) demonstrated that the best results were achieved by organizations whose leaders combined strong drive with personal humility, but some leaders find the idea of humility to be at odds with strong leadership. They think of humility as meekness or weakness and see it as a deficiency, overlooking its real promise.

What if we consider humility in terms of certain behaviors? Because leadership requires working together, what if we consider humility in terms of how we relate to others? Let me define it in a way that is relevant for everyone who leads:

Leader humility is a tendency to feel and display a deep regard for *others' dignity*.

We can still be strong and have high standards. And we can demonstrate respect for others' sense of self-worth.

Leaders Create the Container

Leader humility—supporting others' dignity—improves working together because it is the essential foundation for healthy relationships. Leaders create the *container* for how work is done. A physical container is an object in which we hold, mix, or store something. In a similar way, leaders create the environments or cultures in which we do our work: the people, processes, and practices for how we interact.

Leader humility is the container for healthy relationships with all stakeholders (such as direct reports, coworkers or bosses, legislators, media, vendors, community leaders, or customers). When leaders display humility, a tendency to regard others' dignity as important, the container created for work emphasizes respect for everyone. Interactions become comfortable, and information is freely shared. Because working together is enjoyable, people are motivated to collaborate on shared goals.

When leaders lack humility, when they frequently disregard others' dignity, the container for work becomes unhealthy. Simply put, violating others' dignity harms relationships. Those who feel disrespected become cautious around the leader, sometimes withholding important information if they feel the leader is critical of them. As resentment grows, stakeholders are less inclined to lend their full support. Working together suffers as tensions build. Progress slows and political behavior often grows.

Stakeholders have their own important worries—things like fairness, the amount of change they are being asked to embrace, and their own personal goals. When you think about it, people have three prime questions when facing a new leader (see figure 1). Whether they are asked aloud or merely observed, others evaluate leaders on these dimensions when deciding whether they want to follow along and to what extent.

Curiosity about these questions flows from the observers' personal concerns and is tied to their core sense of dignity, or self-worth. When the answers are favorable, people grow inspired and eager to engage with a leader.

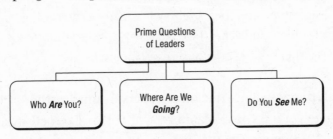

FIGURE 1. Three Prime Questions People Have of Leaders.

Favorable answers allow the leader to connect with the whole person—mind, heart, and spirit—so that people want to join in the quest and give it their all. Yet when the answers are *un*favorable, people tend to withdraw or resist.

Has it always been like this? Were these questions always important? Or has something shifted over the past decade or two?

> The challenge comes from society's expectations of a traditional leader. The top three words that we think of for leaders would include things like "accomplished," "decisive," "strong." We think of leaders as action-oriented, driven, type A people. These are very different times. Leaders are being put more into glass houses than ever before. We are being scrutinized, called to task more, and held accountable. People can go on Glass Door to rate their leader. —PHYLLIS CAMPBELL, CHAIRWOMAN OF JPMORGAN CHASE, PACIFIC NORTHWEST

> I do think it's changing now. There's a lot more focus on transparency in leadership. The presence of the internet is making that happen because people can quickly report what's going on. Because they can tweet or email, we can see inside organizations. So, there's a shift away from being autocratic toward more servant leadership. Still, there are way too many leaders using the older approach. —HOWARD BEHAR, FORMER PRESIDENT OF STARBUCKS COFFEE COMPANY INTERNATIONAL

Is there evidence that most leaders are missing the mark? There is. In a consolidated report, Forbes Councils (Castle 2018) shared results from multiple surveys they had conducted of their communities of prominent executives and entrepreneurs. The results identified leadership as the number three challenge facing business executives (just behind generating revenue and time). Leadership was found to be the single most significant concern by 57 percent of Forbes Human Resources Council, 50 percent of Forbes Nonprofit Council, and 38 percent of Forbes Technology Council. Leadership dominated the concerns among executives in computer and technology industries (36 percent) and was named as the most important concern among VPs (33 percent) and C-suite executives (30 percent). Finally, leadership was identified as the greatest challenge by 42 percent of executives in companies with fifty-one to five hundred employees—a substantial portion of the US private workforce. So, what the executives in Forbes Councils know is that our collective competence in leadership is far below what we need to manage the business challenges at hand.

You might be wondering if this applies to you and how it relates to leader humility. Let me share just two examples of leadership challenges that affect productivity in most organizations: evidence on low employee engagement and turnover costs:

1. In a random sample of more than thirty thousand employees, Gallup (Harter 2018) reported that US employee engagement had risen to 34 percent—still quite low, but the highest level since it began reporting on this. Thirteen percent of employees reported being actively disengaged (indicating miserable work experiences), and 53 percent were "not engaged." In other words, 66 percent of employees were described

as not being "cognitively and emotionally connected to their work and workplace; they will usually show up to work and do the minimum required but will quickly leave their company for a slightly better offer." This results in a huge loss of potential productivity—not only because of the minimal performance of this 66 percent but also because of the negative effect they often have on others' work and the culture in the workplace. The fact that nearly two-thirds of employees are doing the minimum required on their jobs (and are willing to leave) implies that most leaders are not creating healthy containers for working together. Because leader humility is the container for healthy relationships, this poses a significant opportunity: imagine the productivity gain if we could generate even 20 to 30 percent more employee engagement with our collective goals.

2. Talent matters. And attracting and retaining talent is another important leadership issue. McKinsey & Company (2017) reported that top talent can provide a 400 to 800 percent boost in productivity over that of average employees, with the wider gap pertaining to jobs with high complexity (such as software developers, top medical professionals, and managers dealing with complex information or interactions). Yet the best employees have the greatest opportunity to leave. When leaders understand how to recruit and retain talented employees, there is a significant upside benefit. Unfortunately,

many do not recognize the importance of leader humility for this. For example, in a large-scale study of departures, Work Institute (Sears 2017) found that 75 percent of the reason employees leave (including workplace culture and leader behaviors) could have been prevented by managers. In other words, most turnover is caused when leaders create unhealthy containers. This significantly affects the bottom line: Catalyst (2018) estimated turnover costs at $536 billion per year in the United States. This reflects the costs of recruiting, onboarding and training, weak engagement while employed, and loss of productivity from the unfilled role.

In addition to these examples, new demands on business leaders are requiring them to expand their leadership competence. Addressing these effectively will require working together. Economic recovery from the COVID-19 pandemic presents new challenges, as well as new opportunities, as industries reshape themselves. Leaders face dramatically new financial needs and competitive forces, as well as large-scale job displacement and the need for retraining employees. Technologies like artificial intelligence and genetic science also are poised to cause major changes in work and markets in the coming decade. And urgent factors at the interface between business and society are greatly affected by commerce, calling for business leaders who can represent and integrate the interests of all stakeholders. These include the impact of travel on global health, climate change, trade imbalances, wealth disparities (and resulting political instability), globalization of markets and backlash against immigration, and the use (abuse) of communications technology.

Although some challenges affect certain businesses more than others, it will be important for all leaders to guide their organizations in new ways. Some leaders focus so much on analytical factors involved in optimizing profit margins that they neglect the human factors that are actually driving results. And most important is leader humility because it is the container for healthy relationships—for working together effectively. Fortunately, we do see some leaders making progress in this arena:

> On the West Coast, I think we tend to see businesses that align our actions with our values. This has emboldened business leaders to be more values-driven as opposed to simply focusing on shorter-term issues. Airlines are people-based businesses. Investors want high asset utilization and high returns and so forth, and I was drawn to the industry because there is fantastic algebra that a person with an analytical orientation can spend a career optimizing.
>
> But then there's the human side of the business, and that raises the question of which is more important— the algebra or the culture? I think that people have to win. If they feel you have their back, and you give them the tools to work challenges, they will give it their all, and they will help the business prosper and succeed. That is the reason that Alaska is still here while so many other airlines both larger and smaller than us have failed. It's our people. —BRAD TILDEN, CHAIRMAN, PRESIDENT, AND CEO OF ALASKA AIR GROUP

So why aren't more leaders successful? The most promising path to optimizing organizational performance is to get people to align and put their very best energies behind a shared plan. Securing this type of alignment today responds better to leader influence and inspiration than control. Most leaders have vision and drive for results—as well as power. Ordinarily, power is used in one of two ways: through coercion (command and control) or through transaction (rewards and punishment, carrot or stick). This works up to a point but is often limited because people resent being coerced, and they see the transactional approach as somewhat manipulative. Ordinary power can earn the compliance of stakeholders. However, by supporting others' dignity, leader humility is *extraordinarily powerful* for engaging others' hearts and spirits, drawing out their best contributions. Many leaders still emphasize control, because too few understand the power of leader humility to inspire others and navigate the interpersonal dynamics and conflicting opinions on pressing issues. Schein and Schein (2018) called for humble leadership to replace the transactional approach with one that is more personal in order to build more open and trusting relationships.

Creating Gracious Space

Shining a light on this begins by putting ourselves in others' shoes. Think back to the three prime questions people have about leaders: Who Are You, Where Are We Going, and Do You See Me? Rather than relying on command and control to gain support, or the use of fear and intimidation as motivators, leaders with humility create a more gracious space for the dignity of others. By understanding and honoring the needs of others, leaders with humility gain more support because stakeholders become more engaged.

How do humble leaders do this? The answer begins with recognizing that leaders are always being watched by others. *What leaders say and do is scrutinized, and their behavior provides the evidence that answers the three prime questions others have.* In aggregate, the answers to these questions form the impression in others' minds of a leader's humility. So, although my own opinion of my humility is useful, my stakeholders' judgments are critical because their assessment determines how well we will work together.

Recalling the three prime questions people have about leaders, let's consider a mirror image of three prime answers that are provided by leaders. These answers determine whether others find that leader humility exists. Figure 2 previews this relationship and how it affects others' dignity. It shows that, as a leader, my own behaviors signal "Who I Am" (as a person), so these behaviors provide answers to people wanting to know: "Who Are You?" Similarly, "The Direction I Set" (for others to follow) and "How I Treat You" provide answers to questions about "Where Are We Going?" and "Do You See Me?" As will be developed in later chapters, my interactions with you around those prime questions will either support or weaken your sense of dignity, or self-worth.

To the extent that I create a gracious space for your dignity—a healthy container for working together—you will feel enthusiastic and engaged. And if I damage your dignity, odds are good that you will withdraw your support or resist my leadership. My behavior—and your

FIGURE 2. Relationships between Leader Behaviors, Leader Humility, and Others' Dignity.

response to it—will determine how productive we will be together. Therefore, leader humility has a lot to do with how effective a leader can be.

Leader humility, creating a gracious space for others' dignity, is a game changer. It is not the only thing leaders need to do, but it is the critical foundation for working well with others. As a great example of this, consider one of the toughest cases of performance management in business history. The best-selling book *American Icon*, by Bryce Hoffman (2012), chronicles the rescue and turnaround of the Ford Motor Company from near bankruptcy to strong success following the Great Recession of 2008. The hero in this story is Alan Mulally, former president and CEO of Boeing Commercial Airplanes, who took over as CEO of Ford in its decline. Mulally applied a management approach he had developed and used at Boeing, which he calls the Working Together Management System. By using this system, Ford became the only major US automobile manufacturer to survive the threat of bankruptcy during that period without federal bailout money.

Like other strong CEOs, Alan helped Ford craft a compelling vision and comprehensive strategy to move toward success. However, vision and strategy do not go far unless leaders rouse people to join them in implementation. Mulally transformed an organization that was failing (losing $17 billion the year he arrived) into a dynamic one by creating a container for full employee and union engagement with his "One Ford" plan. Along with regular progress reviews, Mulally's specific approach emphasized what he calls "Expected Behaviors." These begin with "People first" and "Everyone is included," and add "Respect, listen, help, and appreciate each other."

Part of the page-turning excitement in Hoffman's book comes from his reports of how Mulally earned the trust of jaded employees because he personally delivered and accepted nothing less than these behaviors from everyone on his team. In a short period of time, Mulally galvanized a company of more than three hundred thousand employees to move Ford from failure to profitability, and he was ranked by *Fortune* as number three among "The World's 50 Greatest Leaders (2014)."

Mulally shares more about the Working Together Management System in chapter 7. He faced *tremendous* challenges as he pursued his leadership goals. Do you relate to any of these issues he experienced that negatively affect performance?

- Weak sales/strained customer relations

- People who do not collaborate when they should

- Lackluster morale among employees

- Leaks to the media about internal problems

- Poor alignment with labor unions and their expectations

- Declining brand reputation

- Challenging government oversight

- Managers who intimidate peers or direct reports

- Unreliable information because people are being self-protective

Mulally's approach of "Everyone is included" showed humility because it acknowledged that others make important contributions and that it takes everyone giving their best to optimize an organization's results. He also showed deep humility by holding himself and the entire leadership team accountable for behaviors that "respect, listen, help, and appreciate others." This created a culture where others' dignity was supported.

Understanding this dynamic is so important that I personally interviewed a select group of twelve current or former presidents and CEOs. My goal is to show that *leader humility is not a minor principle* that works only in rare or unusual places, so I need to show its highly successful use in many organizations you will recognize. Although my sample is small, it is robust.

The CEOs interviewed belong to a somewhat rare set of leaders who are commended by employees, peers, and/or press reports not only for excellence but for leader humility. They represent highly successful companies with global reach and widely recognized brand names. In total, the organizations represented here employ hundreds of thousands of people and manage or generate trillions of dollars of revenue each year. These leaders have significant impact on goods and services we consume,

contribute substantially to our domestic and global economies, and represent a cross section of industries, government, and nonprofit organizations. Their success is
strong evidence that leader humility works.

By default, then, most of these are large businesses.
I could have selected from many smaller companies,
but they would lack the name recognition needed here.
Still, leader humility and working together are relevant
to organizations of any size, and chapter 8 specifically
explains how the principles that work for these large organizations also apply to small and midsized organizations.

The purpose of this book is to illustrate the value of
leader humility. Toward that end, I will be conveying
much advice and experience from each of these exceptional leaders. All quotes from them have been taken
directly from our interviews. I mention their titles and
affiliations only when they are first quoted in the text
in order to minimize repetition; subsequent quotes are
attributed to them by name only. You have already heard
thoughts from three of them in this chapter. Let me provide preliminary introductions to all twelve interviewees in table 1. Chapter 9 briefly shares their exceptional
bios, along with personal statements on how they developed the humility that guides them as leaders. Additional information about each of them is available on
the internet.

We can assume that leaders and aspiring leaders want
to be very effective. And because leaders are typically
high achievers, many want to be exceptional. This book
holds essential information to help them achieve that.
Leader humility improves the employee experience

tremendously. This generates higher levels of employee engagement and performance, and lower turnover. And leader humility helps resolve conflicts and forge consensus across stakeholders. Humility also supports a healthy culture of innovation and safeguards a glowing brand reputation. Humility is, in fact, the secret of great success that so many leaders need.

This basic process of creating a healthy container for working together—a gracious space that supports others' dignity—is so little understood that the next two chapters provide needed explanation. Chapter 2 further explains how humility is a strength, not a weakness. Then it shows humility's potency and provides a model of leader humility. Importantly, leaders can control their own behaviors and improve organizational performance by displaying favorably who they are (admirable character, such as integrity and balanced ego), setting compelling directions (vision and strategy that is for the greater common good), and treating others well (inclusiveness and developmental focus). Chapter 3 provides a deeper understanding of human dignity and why leader humility is so important for great results.

Let's pause to consider the following "Ideas for Action" (a section found at the end of most chapters) to help you apply this material to your own situation. Then, as we proceed, let's draw on the advice and experience of the CEO interviewees listed in table 1.

> ## IDEAS FOR ACTION

1. What is your most pressing leadership challenge?

2. Assess how well you work together with stakeholders:

   a. Make a list of all those affected by your decisions and actions.

   b. Where do you draw the boundary for who is inside and who is outside?

   c. Are all stakeholders included (inside)? If not, what judgment guides your decision that some are outside?

3. Think of two leaders you follow—one you admire and one you don't. In what ways have you wondered about them in ways that relate to the three prime questions (Who Are You? Where Are We Going? Do You See Me?)? How did you respond when the answers seemed favorable? Unfavorable?

4. Consider how your stakeholders evaluate those questions about you. Which stakeholders would answer favorably about you? If some would feel unfavorable, what can you do to improve?

TABLE 1. CEO Interviewees and Affiliations.

NAME	TITLES	ORGANIZATIONS	LOCATIONS
Orlando Ashford	President	Holland America Line	Seattle
Howard Behar	Former president	Starbucks Cofee Company International	Seattle
Phyllis Campbell	Chair	JPMorgan Chase, Pacific Northwest	Seattle, New York
Roger Ferguson	President and CEO	Teachers Insurance and Annuity Association (TIAA)	Washington, DC
Sally Jewell	(a) Former secretary (b) Former CEO	(a) US Department of the Interior (b) REI Corporation	(a) Washington, DC (b) Seattle
Dick Johnson	President and CEO	Foot Locker	New York
Alan Mulally	(a) Former president and CEO (b) Former president and CEO (c) Former president	(a) Ford Motor Company (b) Boeing Commercial Airplanes (c) Boeing Information, Space and Defense Systems	(a) Detroit (b), (c) Seattle
Jeff Musser	CEO	Expeditors International	Seattle
John Noseworthy, MD	Former president and CEO	Mayo Clinic	Minneapolis
Jim Sinegal	Cofounder and former CEO	Costco Wholesale Corporation	Seattle
Brad Tilden	Chairman, president, and CEO	Alaska Air Group	Seattle
Jim Weber	CEO	Brooks Running	Seattle

CHAPTER TWO

The Heart of Humility

A leader's humility allows other people to see that they are important—that they matter.

—Dick Johnson, president and CEO, Foot Locker

After hearing a senior executive's keynote speech, several people commented on how inspiring she was. As they talked about what they had learned from her, I asked if they thought she was a humble leader. One man resisted that idea, saying the speaker *had* to be confident to achieve as much as she had—that women and minorities, especially, can't be too meek but must show strength as leaders to be taken seriously and get ahead. I then asked if he thought the speaker was arrogant. "No. Some of her comments made sure you knew about her accomplishments, but she was light-handed about that. She earned your respect, but she wasn't arrogant." This discussion shows that people can be confused about what leader humility means, so it is important to show how it relates to meekness, confidence, and arrogance.

What Leader Humility Is *Not*

To help clear some of the confusion, let's address first what leader humility is not. Dictionaries typically offer two definitions for humility: one entails meekness and the other indicates the absence of arrogance and excessive pride. Neither definition really communicates what leader humility is. **Let me assure you that leaders with humility can be strong and confident.** And, by avoiding arrogance, they stake out the sweet spot of confidence, as shown in figure 3. Consider this CEO's observation:

> I can see where this could be a complicated question. Some people see humility as being aware of your weaknesses but not necessarily aware of your strengths. In that case, it wouldn't be good for a leader. But there's nothing weak about humility in leadership. It's actually a sign of confidence. When you connect humility in dealing with people with a strong sense of purpose and direction, it's a great superpower for leadership.
>
> Arrogance is not the same and should not be confused with confidence. Arrogance overwhelms others and shuts them down. Confidence creates a frame or umbrella of leadership that guides people. Often, arrogance reflects serious insecurities, while confidence can suggest steadfast, informed conviction. Business is a team sport, and teams always do best when people give their all in an environment of trust and support.
>
> —JIM WEBER, CEO, BROOKS RUNNING

In a similar vein, Morris, Brotheridge, and Urbanski (2005, 1331) defined humility as "that crest of human excellence between arrogance and lowliness." Figure 3 depicts this relationship; below, I explain how humility relates to meekness and arrogance.

FIGURE 3. Leader Humility in Context of Common Terms.

Leader Humility Is *Not* Meekness

The idea of humility as meekness has faith-based origins. Some studies interpret humility as a view of oneself that assumes something greater than oneself exists (Ou et al. 2014). This may imply a belief in God or a specific religious doctrine that suggests humbling oneself before a higher power. But meekness is not always faith based. It can reflect a cultural upbringing that discouraged asserting one's views—or personality factors like general shyness or a lack of confidence.

Regardless of the cause, when people think of humility only as meekness, it's easy to see this as inappropriate for leadership. Leaders with humility need to be confident and strong enough to set direction, take reasonable risks, and bear responsibility. They need to appreciate their skills and accomplishments—and recognize their limitations. Leader humility does not imply meekness.

There is a thin line between confidence and conceit. A person in a large job of leadership has to walk that line. You must have confidence, but you can't cross the line. I know what I know, and I know what I *don't* know—and I'm very comfortable with both. It's impossible to know everything in business today. If I meet a leader like that, I short that stock! I have to know my limitations. Otherwise, I put the organization at risk by making decisions where I don't know what I'm doing.

—ORLANDO ASHFORD, PRESIDENT, HOLLAND AMERICA LINE

Absence of Arrogance

The other common definition of humility—the absence of arrogance and excessive pride—is relevant to leader humility (but does not fully define leader humility). Let's first see how it is relevant. Among the CEOs interviewed, this comment sums it up well and is illustrated in figure 4:

> Arrogance is like a cancer. It permeates the whole organization. It's a horrible thing. Actions speak for themselves. You don't need braggadocio. Humility is necessary. —JIM SINEGAL, COFOUNDER AND FORMER CEO, COSTCO WHOLESALE CORPORATION

Arrogance is a turnoff for many (perhaps most) people. Excessive pride overshadows the value and accomplishments of others. If a leader's ego is too big, he or she will have trouble gaining commitment and broad support from those who are needed for success (peers, employees, other stakeholders). Arrogant leaders signal their sense of superiority through behaviors like the following:

- Persistent name-dropping

- Cutting people off in conversation

- Excessive displays of status and perk

- Insulting, bullying, or being condescending to others

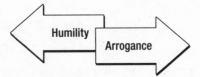

FIGURE 4. Direction of Humility
Compared with Arrogance.

- Taking credit for others' work

- Blaming or refusing to accept responsibility for their own mistakes

- Frequently boasting about themselves (or friends, family, successes)

Arrogant leaders tend to rely on power and commands to get the work done. This creates a climate of fear and intimidation. If leaders can exert direct control, this may succeed. Even then, while followers may comply, they will dislike being treated this way because it trivializes their own dignity. Often they will resist the leader's direction by limiting their productivity, leaking negative information to the media, or leaving the organization. So, arrogance should be avoided, and humble leaders are not arrogant. Yet defining humility as the absence of excessive pride or arrogance fails to show its real power in leadership.

What Leader Humility *Is*

If leader humility is not meekness or arrogance, then what *is* it? Some authors suggest that humility shows up in our interactions with others, based on our perspective about ourselves and the relationship (Nielsen, Marrone, and Ferraro 2014). Others observe that humble people seem to lack an excessive focus on themselves (Hess and Ludwig 2017; Nielsen and Marrone 2018). These authors frame humility as being related to how we see ourselves and how we see others. But what *is* that exactly? What is *present* when others see a leader's humility as opposed to what is absent? Can we state what is present in a way that is practical for leaders, while being consistent with existing definitions and writing about humility?

Regard for Others' Dignity

I define leader humility as **a tendency to *feel* and *display* a deep regard for others' dignity.*** The word *regard* implies respect or admiration; it is derived from the French verb *regarder*, which means to take notice of, look at, observe. While arrogance is self-focused and often insensitive to others, humility is other-focused and emphasizes recognition and support for others' dignity. Thrive Global (Davis 2018) noted that "those who have cultivated humility . . . go from being consumed with themselves (an inner focus) to looking for ways to contribute and help others (an outer focus)."

Humble leaders are aware of their strengths but also realize they can't know everything. With a secure sense of self, humble leaders tend to respect others' dignity, regardless of others' rank and position. This value for the dignity of others governs the leader's speech and actions quite differently than what we see in arrogant

---

* Although there is growing academic interest in the topic of humility, leader humility as a scholarly construct is not well developed. This book's practitioner focus does not support construct differentiation and validation. However, organizational research would benefit from robust assessment of the proposed definition of leader humility and from empirical exploration of the forthcoming model, especially in field versus lab studies.

leaders. Leaders with humility are not merely neutral—not merely avoiding a negative state (arrogance). They display a positive or affirmative stance toward (that is, genuinely caring about) others' dignity:

> Fundamentally, you actually can't think you are better
> than other people. Your mindset and attitude have to
> be that we're all human, we all make mistakes, and we
> come from different backgrounds and perspectives.
> —BRAD TILDEN

I added the element of feeling, an emotional state, in defining leader humility for two reasons. First, it is hard to fake this. Feeling affects our nonverbal communication, which has long been considered to comprise 93 percent of communication (Mehrabian 1972). We take cues about what others think of us from tone of voice, body language, eye movement, and facial expression, which are less subject to conscious control than our speech. And when nonverbal cues conflict with verbal speech, we rely on nonverbal cues most heavily to interpret what others really mean. Equally important: a tendency to feel regard for others' dignity generates reasonably consistent behaviors (displaying a deep regard) that affirm the value of others. In practice, it is a humble person's desire to affirm the dignity of others that suppresses arrogance.

Extraordinarily Powerful

Earlier, I mentioned that leaders have power. They vary in how they use it. What might be considered an *ordinary* use of power (that is, still quite common) involves command and control, carrot or stick. Sometimes it stresses dominance over others through fear and intimidation.

Those may work to an extent but come at a price. Consider these perspectives:

> Leaders can be effective even if they're not humble.
> But it's different. I met with a well-known oil company
> executive when I was secretary of the interior. He was
> very arrogant and clearly had a successful career. I was
> having a thoughtful discussion with leading oil indus-
> try CEOs from around the world when this man walked
> in the room. His arrogance took over at that point, and
> the ability to have a respectful dialogue ceased. He
> showed a total lack of willingness to listen to the group
> or figure out what was going on. It was clear that the
> group was intimidated by his presence, and we lost the
> value of our discussion that may have prevailed through
> a more respectful approach. —SALLY JEWELL, FORMER
> SECRETARY, US DEPARTMENT OF THE INTERIOR, AND FORMER CEO,
> REI CORPORATION

> The interesting thing about arrogant, autocratic leader-
> ship is that it only works to a point. It doesn't draw peo-
> ple in. People don't stay in those environments unless
> they feel they have to—or unless it's for the money.
> [I]n many cases they leave part of themselves at home
> and don't fully connect in . . . you will only get what
> you ask for and no more. . . . You do see the domineer-
> ing style in politics at times, but elections are episodic.
> Nothing in great businesses is episodic—you *must*
> deliver repeat performances—year in, year out. To do
> that, you must draw people in. —JIM WEBER

The downside of using ordinary power is that it is actually rather limited for motivating people: it draws compliance, not full engagement. Because humility involves

showing deep regard for others' dignity, it goes beyond ordinary power. It is *extraordinarily* powerful because when we support the dignity of others, we inspire them and boost their enthusiasm for us as leaders. Humility engages their hearts, minds, and spirits. And when people are energized and fully engaged, their creative and productive contributions soar. But don't just take my word for it:

> I don't think you keep the best people or get the best energy from them if you don't have a culture that's feeding them, reinforcing their superpowers, and challenging them. We're playing a long game, and we know that, over time, you can't compete with a strong culture. We are holding on to talent because they can see a work environment that welcomes them and allows them to make an impact.
>
> Command-and-control leaders don't keep their best people. They also will model and inbreed selfishness over time. If you look at Brooks's results, we have had three major pivot points: 2001, 2009, and 2017. In this recent strategy reset, we've come out of it with rapid growth, up 30 percent+ in the first half of [2018]. I know our success is very much an outcome of our culture, values, and people. Over time, it's our culture and purpose-driven strategy that will be a force multiplier for Brooks. —JIM WEBER

Leader humility, then, is a competitive advantage today. Strategically, it makes good business sense, and it is seen as a strength by many leaders who are also quite confident and successful.

Needed: A Model of Leader Humility

Let me close with some context and a brief review, then pull it all together. The context for humility making a compelling difference in leadership results was shown by Collins (2001), who found that leaders with strong drive (fierce resolve) coupled with personal humility are the ones who lead organizations to greatness. Studies have since shown that humility enhances a number of personal, learning, and organizational outcomes (see, for example, Nielsen and Marrone 2018 for a comprehensive review). Most leaders are selected for their roles because they were outstanding achievers, so we assume that most have strong drive. Yet the need for personal humility is often neglected when selecting leaders, and the absence of it can seriously limit their effectiveness.

Chapter 1 introduced three questions people ask themselves about leaders: Who Are You? Where Are We Going? Do You See Me? It indicated that leader interactions around those three questions would either support or weaken others' dignity, or self-worth. This chapter explained that leader humility is neither meekness nor merely an absence of arrogance. Instead, I defined humility pragmatically for leaders as a tendency to feel and display a deep regard for others' dignity. And a leader's humility has a lot to do with how effective a leader can be: supporting dignity increases the chance that people feel enthusiastic and engaged, and damaging others' dignity causes people to limit their support or resist leadership.

Given the importance of leader humility, we need to identify specific behaviors that support others' dignity. As shown in figure 5, there are six keys to leader humility: balanced ego and robust integrity (related to "Who

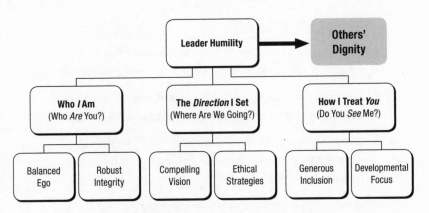

FIGURE 5. Six Keys to Leader Humility.

I Am"), compelling vision and ethical strategies ("The Direction I Set"), and generous inclusion and developmental focus ("How I Treat You"). I call these keys that open a lock. When we use the right key and turn it in the right way, the lock opens. If we don't have the right key, the lock won't budge. In a similar way, we affect others' dignity positively by using these six keys well.

The behaviors related to each of these keys will be explained in chapters 4 through 6. But first, let's consider ideas for action. Then I'll clarify more fully what human dignity is and why it is so important for leaders to honor it—the subject of chapter 3.

IDEAS FOR ACTION

1. On a 5-point scale, with 5 meaning very high and 1 meaning very low, how do you rate your confidence?

2. On a continuum running from meekness at one end to arrogance at the other, where do you place yourself?

3. On a 5-point scale, with 5 meaning very high and 1 meaning very low, how do you rate your personal regard for others' dignity?

4. Which of the six keys to leader humility do you think are your strongest? Are any of them weak? If so, pay particular attention to the chapters describing those keys.

CHAPTER THREE

The Deal with Dignity

The most luxurious possession, the richest treasure
anybody has, is his personal dignity.
—Jackie Robinson

Good business strategy must center on people because stakeholders have a vested interest: they can take action, in one way or another, based on their approval or disapproval of what leaders do. So, a top concern for leaders needs to be creating a healthy container for working together with all stakeholders: customers/clients, employees, shareholders, community citizens, regulators, supply-chain constituents, board members, peers, bosses, and even the press. This container includes both the internal cultures we create *and* the external goals we pursue.

> [Y]ou must think long-term. Short-term thinking promotes more self-centered or unilateral decisions. In the long term, actions based on humility drive greater return on investment. . . . We need to recognize the importance of considering stakeholder good as opposed to just shareholder value. Shareholder value leads to a transactional view of people—people are just there to achieve profit and shareholder returns. Stakeholder good

is a broader view of people (e.g., customers, employees,
suppliers), and it takes humility to value that.
—PHYLLIS CAMPBELL

Successfully addressing stakeholder relationships
begins with recalling two fundamental truths and how
they apply to leadership. First, leaders hold *power* to ini-
tiate, influence, and implement. Organizational power
often involves control: leaders may hire and terminate
employees, allocate assignments and resources, convene
meetings for accountability, evaluate performance, and
provide emotional support (or blame) when challenges
arise. Beyond the organization, leaders, collectively, make
decisions that show their power to select suppliers, affect
communities (lobbying and legislating, opening or clos-
ing plants), and impact the environment (sustainable or
nonsustainable practices), for example. Some leaders are
quite aware of their power; others seem to barely consider
it. Some leaders relish power for personal use. Enjoying
the perks that go with power, they ensure that others
recognize this and defer to them. Other leaders seem to
prefer to use their power for the greater good, focusing
less on themselves and more on serving the organization
and society as best they can.

Regardless of the extent to which leaders recognize
their power, danger arises when it is misused. And abuse
of power most often comes from ignorance of—or bla-
tant disregard for—a second fundamental principle that
leaders need to fully understand:

**Every human being has and needs a
sense of self-worth—of dignity.**

Because most people try to maintain a positive sense of self-worth, leaders who interact in ways that honor others' dignity will be most effective. If they violate others' dignity—seriously and/or repeatedly—leaders will be far less effective.

Why Is Dignity Important?

Dignity implies that each person is worthy of honor and respect for who he or she is, regardless of status or accomplishment. Because dignity refers to *intrinsic* human worth, it can neither be earned nor taken away. Still, a person's dignity can be violated when behaviors of others fail to recognize and honor it. Some practices represent gross violations of human dignity (such as torture, rape, slavery). But we need to recognize that dignity is also violated in subtler ways. This can happen in casual, social interactions, yet it is even more serious when coupled with power—such as when we lead.

Subtle violations often flow from arrogance when one person presumes superiority over another. And violations can be caused by structures and policies that grow from a *shared* sense of arrogance (a broadly held sense of superiority among members of one group about another group). A few examples of these violations in the workplace are sexual harassment, discrimination in hiring and promotion, bullying, verbal condescension, excessive criticism, and other displays of arrogance. Unfortunately, many of these latter practices are common among leaders—and their negative impact is serious because offensive behavior is also coupled with power.

Whether intentional or not, when leaders behave in these ways, they fundamentally violate another's *dignity*.

Because those on the receiving end of offensive behavior are not equal in power, they may not challenge the leader overtly (for example, consider the many delayed claims of sexual harassment that became evident during the #MeToo movement). Yet, the leader's behavior will cause resentment, anger, or withdrawal—as opposed to empowerment, engagement, and enthusiasm. This is why an understanding of human dignity and leader humility is so important.

Human dignity itself is not a new concept, but times have changed. In the past, people were more accommodating of autocratic (and even condescending) leadership. Today, more people are educated and aware, mindful of human rights and sensitive to mistreatment as employees, consumers, and citizens.

> A lot of work today also requires employees who are highly skilled or highly educated. They expect to be treated respectfully. It takes humility to do that. The younger generation also expects someone they can talk to who will listen to them and be compassionate. So, humility in leadership is important. I sometimes meet executives from other companies and am surprised at how they got where they are because they are so disrespectful. —JEFF MUSSER, CEO, EXPEDITORS INTERNATIONAL

Travel, media, and well-known litigation have helped the public recognize when dignity is being supported or violated. Because we expect to be heard and to have our views respected, there is a much greater requirement for leaders to use power gently—to be able to engage with us around our needs and to forge consensus out of our conflicting views. Indeed, one of the prime responsibilities in leadership is that of orchestrating and respectfully managing conversations that are difficult or contentious. Unfortunately, many leaders have lagged in adjusting their use of power. They take leadership to mean obtaining an advantage over others, sometimes through arrogance or dominance based on presumed superiority:

> Arrogance denigrates performance in any organization. People think arrogant, autocratic leadership enhances performance, but it doesn't. You lose people—good people. There's no trust. People look over their shoulder when there's no trust. They worry about protecting themselves. So, it's hard to have a dynamic organization. And turnover is high. People only stay out of fear. If the economy is bad, they may stay, but as soon as it improves, they are gone. —HOWARD BEHAR

There is significant advantage to be gained from supporting the dignity of various groups as opposed to over-dominating or trying to win a position in the short term. To support human dignity, leaders first need a clear understanding of what goes into another's sense of dignity. Then they can see how a leader's humility affects dignity during interactions.

Unpacking Dignity

Human dignity stems from our identity. It rests on cultural values we hold about the sanctity of life, as well as feelings we have about our individual, personal qualities. Thus, it consists of both basic and personal (or unique) components.

Basic Component

At its most basic, human dignity rests on our cultural beliefs in the sanctity of life itself. Many faith traditions and laws promote the notion that life is to be valued and protected. Murder is considered wrong, and we have ongoing debates about the right to life of the unborn, the cruelty of capital punishment, the tragedy of suicide, and, relatedly, the appropriateness of choosing to end one's life during terminal illness. We have further laws and policies that protect children, for example, knowing that children are vulnerable. These policies would not exist if we did not fundamentally value human life—as contrasted with our weaker laws protecting animal welfare.

We grow up with a basic sense that our lives are valuable simply because we exist. This belief then extends to policies and expectations around the decency of work, such as the responsibility of employers to provide safe and healthy work environments. Finally, we expect leaders to show reasonable compassion for many human issues that affect work, such as illness or major loss, and the current pressure that employers are facing to provide paid parental leave. All of these practices extend from the basic component of our dignity: human life itself is to be valued. This component is the foundation of our dignity. On top of it, each of us builds a larger, much more personal, edifice.

Personal Component

The personal (or unique) component of dignity consists of elements that differentiate one person from another. These are aspects of our identity that make us unique *and* about which we feel pride or discomfort. Examples may include the following:

- Demographic characteristics (such as race, gender, age)

- Talents and achievements

- Family structure and belonging

- Group or tribal membership (nationality, faith, other strong affiliation)

- Economic status

- Values, culture, and subculture

- Language

- Physical appearance (such as height, weight, skin color, tattoos, hair texture)

- Sexual orientation and identity

Let me offer just one poignant example. Mia came home from school very upset one afternoon. She told her mother, Cecily, that the teacher, while trying to be supportive, had made repeated reference to Mia as being from a broken family. There was indeed no father in the home, so the teacher had made some assumptions. Cecily called a meeting with the teacher to let her know that she had upset Mia and to inform her that, as a single adult, Cecily had opted to become pregnant by artificial insemination because she wanted to be a mother. Cecily said, "Our family is not 'broken.' It has been intact as the two of us since the day Mia was born."

I chose this example because it can be controversial— and that is the point. It doesn't matter what our judgments are; it is others' dignity that is important. While the teacher's assumptions about a broken home may have been reasonable, Mia had as much right as other children to feel proud of her family structure, and her sense of dignity was hurt. The teacher, who held a classroom leadership role, needed to change her behavior to support the personal component of this child's dignity.

A full list of specific examples would be nearly endless, which is why we need to embrace humility. Leader humility provides direction that we should support others' dignity; as a principle for healthy relationships, humility guides the actions and responses we need to demonstrate in specific situations. As with this teacher, we all face situations in which we make mistakes. That is human, but how we respond is part of the container we create for working together. Fortunately, the teacher apologized to Cecily and Mia and became more thoughtful about judgments she placed on others and how the words we use often hold negative implications.

Each of us has need for a positive sense of self-worth—and *we each get to define what about ourselves we consider worthy*. We tend to hold positive views about traits we have that are broadly valued in society (such as intelligence or attractiveness). We may also hold positive views about personal qualities that others do not view as favorably (such as our race, gender, height, family structure, or faith). And we hold sensitivities or shame about other qualities we have (perhaps excess weight, an accent, a weakness or limitation). Wherever we have positive or negative feelings about our personal qualities, if others disparage those qualities, our dignity takes a hit. And many of us will feel that hit whether comments are made directly to us or about others who share similar traits. If I have blond hair and someone makes "dumb blonde" jokes, my dignity is hit even though being blond is generally considered a positive trait. Likewise, if I struggle with trying to lose twenty pounds and someone comments that overweight people are lazy and self-indulgent, my dignity takes a hit.

What offends one person may not offend another. This may be partly because of personal sensitivity (sometimes the case—but not always). When we are surprised that our comments or behavior have offended another, it is easy to assume that the person is just too sensitive. But notice that when we assume others are too sensitive and should not have been offended, we grant superiority to our own judgment over the other's reaction. The risk in doing this is that we may not question our own behavior when perhaps we should.

Our comments or behavior may, in fact, be offensive if people feel strongly about the particular trait we criticized. If it was not very important to their sense of self-worth, they might shrug off a negative comment. But if it is a source of deep pride or discomfort, they will feel the hit. Also, one joke by itself may not cause harm, but repeated jokes or negative comments made by the same person or with a seriously disparaging tone can damage the relationship. And if society often denigrates certain personal characteristics (race, faith, age, weight), sensitivity may well be justified. This is why it is so important not to make jokes at others' expense. It is more helpful to try to understand why others have specific sensitivities— as we all do—and respect them.

Interacting with Others' Dignity

Understanding that dignity has a very personal component may ease some of the confusion about political correctness and resentment over being challenged for comments we make. Our culture is expanding in its diversity. We can respond to this in one of two ways. The first is from an attitude of superiority that implies, "I am better than you and get to decide what is valuable or unworthy about you—and you had better just take it." In power dominance models, this may work. People may comply because they have to—but they are not likely to do so wholeheartedly.

The other approach is to recognize that all individuals have the right to define what they feel is worthy about themselves. We *all* have and need dignity—a sense of self-worth—and no one's dignity (including my own) is superior to another's. Yet, as a leader of people, I am responsible for honoring *others'* dignity because I create the container for working together. Hicks (2018, 16–17) described honoring dignity in terms of practices that include acceptance of identity, recognition (of talents and hard work), inclusion, and accountability for your own actions when you violate others' dignity. This raises three important questions.

> First, how does dignity fit into competition, winning, and notions of merit? Can't I feel pride for what I have accomplished? Absolutely. Our accomplishments are part of our own sense of self-worth. It is totally appropriate for us to feel proud of what we have achieved—and to share that at times with close associates. But, if we frequently flaunt our achievements around others

who lack them, we do risk offending their dignity. And, if we conclude that we are fundamentally better than others because of our accomplishments, we will find a lot of disbelievers. All of us have a package of strengths and weaknesses. People may admire us for some of our strengths, but that doesn't mean they believe they are less worthy for their own attributes. Because leaders have power, those who wield it with an air of superiority may gain compliance—while earning disdain. All leaders need to recognize and acknowledge the genuine worth of others.

The second question that arises around honoring others' dignity concerns misbehavior. What about illegal or destructive behavior? Am I supposed to support someone's choice to do the wrong thing? Honoring dignity does not require supporting lawlessness or destructive behavior. Dignity is strictly about our sense of human worth. Most democracies have legal structures that attempt to honor dignity even as they judge and punish bad behavior. Examples include rules around arrest and detention, standards of evidence, and jury trials. These practices derive from ideals of human rights and dignity—while still holding individuals accountable to our laws.

Finally, you might wonder about standards of performance. Does honoring others' dignity mean we can't hold people responsible? Standards are fine, and honoring dignity does not prevent acting on poor performance. When we communicate standards and give feedback on how someone's performance is measuring up, we are actually supporting his or her dignity by being clear about expectations that lead to success. Strong human resource policies emphasize setting goals and standards and evaluating performance—not personalities. The important thing is to focus on how others' performance compares with the standards we set—and not to suggest that a shortfall makes them lesser human beings. No one is good at everything. We can still signal that we value the person, but the performance needs to improve, or we will need to take corrective action.

In sum, *honoring others' dignity begins with acknowledging that each of us is one of a kind, and we each have a unique sense of self-worth.* Although we share much in common with others, the elements that distinguish us are many. When societies are largely homogeneous, characteristics that diverge from dominant group norms are often ignored or disrespected, yet few people speak up because their numbers are small. However, as countries have become multicultural and more varied socially and economically, those who are not part of the dominant group tend to be less willing to allow those in power to disrespect and marginalize them for their differences. Instead we see an evolving social acceptance of many differences (and many intersections among them).

This change also explains why so many leaders find it harder and more complex than it used to be to work with people. How can leaders possibly accommodate all these differences and expectations? There tend to be three responses to this dilemma:

1. Some leaders encourage cultural assimilation. They trivialize or discount the value of these unique differences, asking others to adapt entirely (versus merely when essential) to the dominant culture. Yet doing so is arrogant (it takes a sense of superiority to decide that another's unique qualities should *not* be considered important to them)—and is likely to violate another's sense of dignity.

2. Somewhat differently, other leaders feel burdened by so many different views that they try to ignore them. They openly accept that there are differences, but they don't recognize or consider how these affect organizational outcomes (for example, how diverse team members have helpful insights for customer-facing businesses, or that different stakeholder groups have different, yet valid, concerns). These leaders simply drive action toward their goals or toward achieving a specific advantage—as if one size will fit all. This can invite backlash, failures during implementation, breakdowns in negotiation, and political stalemates.

3. What is genuinely needed is the third approach: humility.

The last chapter introduced a model of leader humility. The next three chapters will explore this model in depth. Chapter 4 discusses balanced ego and integrity as being critical as leaders convey "Who I Am." Chapter 5 is devoted to compelling vision and ethical strategies that show "The Direction I Set." And chapter 6 reveals that generous inclusion and developmental focus are central concerns in "How I Treat You." Mastering these six keys will enhance any leader's competence and contribute to great success.

IDEAS FOR ACTION

1. Consider the elements of dignity listed as examples in the "Personal Component" section of this chapter. How variable are your stakeholders and on which dimensions?

2. Select three of your key stakeholders, and try to identify the elements of personal dignity you believe mean a lot to each of them. Have you ever noticed sensitivities in them that support your beliefs?

3. As a leader, how comfortable are you with diversity? What assumptions do you make about people's backgrounds?

4. Do your personal judgments about stakeholders affect your ability to support their dignity?

CHAPTER FOUR

Who I Am

*Nearly all men can stand adversity, but if you want
to test a man's character, give him power.*

—Abraham Lincoln

When people first meet us, they want to know who we are. Who is the person behind the name? This natural curiosity applies to leaders in a more penetrating way because leaders have power and influence. Two of the most important aspects of who you are that affect others' dignity are how your ego appears when you interact with people and the level of integrity you display. These are shown in figure 6 as keys to "Who I Am."

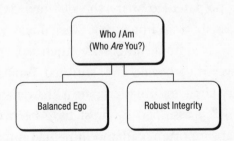

FIGURE 6. Keys to "Who I Am."

These two keys have a lot to do with how a leader uses power because ego and integrity reflect a leader's personal sense of him- or herself in relation to others. As leaders vary a lot on these dimensions, let's look at each in turn.

Balanced Ego

Ego is commonly defined as our opinion of ourselves, especially of our own importance or ability. It refers to a person's sense of "I"—the conscious self that thinks, feels, and exercises will. A common way that people judge leaders' egos is to watch how we wear the trappings of power. People's judgments are formed by observing the leader interacting with others and from direct, personal interaction. Judgments about the leader may arise over time or, occasionally, from a compelling experience. An example of the latter was my first encounter with Jim Sinegal:

> Newly hired to run the Executive Leadership Program at Seattle University, I needed to arrange an executive speaker on short notice. Exploring possibilities, I reached out to Sinegal, cofounder and CEO of Costco Wholesale. I placed a phone call, prepared to share the planned date with his assistant and hear that Sinegal was unavailable. The phone rang once, then a firm voice answered, "Sinegal." I was stunned. What CEO of a very large, multinational firm answers his own phone?! I assumed he must have been expecting an important call and mine had interceded. Unprepared for this, I nervously explained who I was and that, although he didn't know me, I'd

like him to speak to our class. He replied briskly, "What's the date again? What time? And what's your phone number? I'll have to check my calendar and get back to you." I was certain I was being handed off to an assistant, who would call back regretting Jim's unavailability to speak.

I'd begun wondering who else I could ask, when fifteen minutes later my phone rang. The voice on the other end said, "Marilyn, this is Jim Sinegal. The date looks OK. Where is it and what time do you need me there?" I was stunned again. He not only agreed to my request but had meant what he said about checking his calendar—then he personally called me back! Sometime later, on hearing me retell this story, Jim added, "Well, I don't always answer my own phone, Marilyn. But if I'm sitting there free, I do."

Despite the fact that we had not met, Sinegal's behavior minimized the status difference between us. This display of balanced ego showed deep regard for my dignity. He certainly could have had someone else answer his phone or call me back—I would have been neither surprised nor disappointed. Many perks that come with executive positions, such as having an assistant to manage phone calls and scheduling, are designed to help leaders get more work done. But Sinegal's gesture of returning my call himself was an unexpected, personal touch. It told me I mattered to him—that he saw me not as an intrusion in his very busy day but as a human being who deserved his regard and honesty. From this compelling exchange, I sensed Jim Sinegal's balanced ego and I felt *seen*.

We do notice whether leaders emphasize or minimize the status difference between us. Leaders with a balanced ego are aware of their power but confident enough in themselves that they prefer to minimize its unnecessary display:

> People appreciate leadership humility even in senior leaders. A lot of times, I'll get asked about my work. People usually ask first about what I do, and I'll say I work for Holland America. They might then ask what I do there, and I'll say I'm in senior management. If they come at it a third time, they might ask what job and I'll tell them CEO, but I usually won't start there.
> —ORLANDO ASHFORD

Excessive Status Displays

In contrast with balanced ego, leaders who display high ego tend to emphasize their status in a number of ways, like ensuring that their formal title is widely known and used, that the perks of their position are broadly visible, and that others kowtow to them. They often use support services to do simple or personal tasks even when they could do the tasks on their own. They may minimize association with, or show disdain for, people who are below them in rank. Enjoying the feeling of power from having their opinions reinforced, they tend to tolerate little disagreement and surround themselves with yes-men. Leaders like this are seen by others as displaying high ego and, thus, a lack of humility. Their behaviors are self-focused (or even disrespectful of others) and these leaders harm others' dignity by hoisting their own sense of self-worth above that of others. While some people admire the strongman model of leadership, many people today do not. People generally see high displays of ego as deeply disregarding others' dignity. And a leader's lack of humility hinders working together:

> Humility is a *strength*. It's really having confidence in yourself, so you don't have to put on a façade. And strength in leadership is not at odds with humility. Being humble is not the same as being soft. You can have very high standards and still be humble. But, at the end of the day, I realize that I'm not the one who actually delivers the results—it's other people who accomplish them. I play a role of getting people together to drive results. So, humility is important in doing that.
> —JEFF MUSSER

Arrogance and Self-Promotion

Regardless of whether they emphasize status differences, some leaders will be seen as lacking in balanced ego because they display arrogance. As indicated in chapter 2, arrogance may show up as frequent name-dropping, boasting about personal accomplishments, or making condescending or insulting comments to others that signal they are less important. Sometimes arrogant leaders, seeing themselves as the center of the organization's success, take credit for work that actually was shared by many—and blame others or refuse to take personal responsibility for their own mistakes. While arrogance can be annoying in social contexts, it is much worse among leaders—because it is coupled with power.

This may seem like a paradox because people often need to promote themselves in order to be seen and

selected into leadership positions. To distinguish themselves from the crowd and advance in their careers, they
typically need to display strong confidence and make
sure that others know about their accomplishments. The
confusion is resolved by understanding that we are seen
differently when we *have* power. The presence of power
makes people even more concerned with who we are. So,
once power is in hand, leaders need to dial back their
display of ego and focus more on others.

> Humility is *not* meekness or the opposite of strength,
> but it does mean being void of arrogance. It means I am
> not afraid. I am self-confident and can engage in dia-
> logue and not debates. Humility means having a modest
> view of one's importance, not thinking you are better,
> being down to earth. It also means understanding that
> there are universal needs, that "that man" is you, that
> all of us have human value. C. S. Lewis said that humil-
> ity is not thinking less of yourself but thinking of your-
> self less. —ALAN MULALLY, FORMER PRESIDENT AND CEO, FORD
> MOTOR COMPANY AND BOEING COMMERCIAL AIRPLANES, AND
> FORMER PRESIDENT, BOEING INFORMATION, DEFENSE AND SPACE
> SYSTEMS

Self-Awareness
Having a balanced ego requires self-awareness. Leaders
need an accurate sense of the strengths they bring to the
context but also need to know when and how to modulate
their behaviors—when to lead, when to listen, when to
step back and encourage others to move forward. Gaining
this requires a certain vulnerability. Leaders can't know
everything and can often learn from others in the organization—even from those who are younger, newer, or
lower in status, or who come from diverse professional or

cultural backgrounds. Leaders with humility are confident enough to be vulnerable. They are open to feedback, as well as able to admit their limitations and mistakes.

> As a CEO, it's true that you must have a certain ego strength to lead and survive. But practicing medicine has taught me other things. As a neurologist, specifically, I've seen the courage of patients and families in dealing with complex, confusing, and often tragic illnesses. I've come to realize the limitations we have in being able to help, and that builds humility. I've learned that I have some abilities and lack others. I'm often not the smartest person in the room. If I want to get something done, it helps to surround myself with those who have skills I don't have. Our system of regular, disciplined feedback also has helped me. I once articulated a vision and thought I had been open. What I didn't realize was that there were a lot of people who didn't feel I was open. I hadn't realized I was debating them; I wasn't listening. My coach said, "Share that realization with the team, and tell them you're working on it. Then check back and ask how you're doing." —JOHN NOSEWORTHY, MD, FORMER PRESIDENT AND CEO, MAYO CLINIC

Equally important to being open is a willingness to *seek out critical feedback* and accept it. We all need truth tellers in our lives. No one gets to be successful without mentors or coaches. And the higher that leaders go in their careers, the more they need this feedback. Paradoxically, as leaders rise in status, there are many people who try to shield them from news that is not good and fewer people who are willing to be truth tellers. Humble leaders are aware that because they hold power, there tend to be gatekeepers or palace guards around them.

Realizing they need people who can give them critical feedback, leaders with humility make a genuine effort to get it:

> In positions of power, there is increased risk that a leader is told what people believe they want to hear, not what people actually believe. The higher someone is in power, the more [people] curate the information they provide you. Seeking and listening to genuine feedback is essential in enabling leaders to address challenges before they become serious. When I was at REI and visiting a retail store, I generally made a beeline to the cashiers, the bike shop, the storeroom and warehouse area. I wanted to greet and listen to people who worked throughout the store. It shows respect, of course, but it's also a great place for insight. The farther from power people are, the more willing they are to talk. I believe in connecting with people at all levels of the organization, demonstrating a genuine willingness to listen and take action. —SALLY JEWELL

Robust Integrity

Integrity means being honest and having strong moral principles. This pertains first to the leader's personal conduct. Although some people will ignore a leader's immorality, many others are offended. Poor integrity shows disregard for others' dignity because many people's sense of self-worth includes values of honesty and doing the right thing. Because they expect integrity from themselves, they don't want to follow or associate with people who lack it. Leaders show humility (regard for others' dignity) by behaving in ways that reflect a high standard of personal conduct, not only in their work but also in their personal lives.

In the context of work, integrity lends reliability to a leader's words and actions. It implies that the leader is authentic and honest in communication, ensuring that actions are consistent with words. This includes timely responses to inquiries and follow-through on appointments and expected communication. It allows others to trust that what they are hearing is true, that they can depend on what the leader says, and that the leader has integrity in his or her personal standards of work.

Is perfection required? In truth, leaders handle complex situations and are often faced with tradeoffs. Public relations are also a reality. Seeking perfection in human life all but guarantees disappointment. But integrity should be robust—very strong. Leaders need to anchor their words and actions in the same values they publicly state. They need to know where the honest line in the sand is and stay on the proper side of it. And while expecting perfection may be unrealistic, some leaders confuse truth with excessive spin—or lie outright and often. They underestimate others' ability to see through misinformation or misdeeds. Frequent or serious integrity outages are offensive to many, and lack of integrity damages working together.

> Leaders need to know who they are—and how others
> see them—and measure that against what are eight to
> ten core values . . . like caring, love, giving trust before
> you get it. So, we have to really decide what these things
> mean to us. Values are not what I or anyone says, but
> what we actually *do*. . . . [H]ow do my values inform

decisions and what I do? How do they inform what I want out of life?

One of the frustrations I have is watching people support politicians who lie and insult people, but say they support them for their policies. I'll ask, "So do you value honesty and kindness to people?" They'll say yes but not realize their *actions* say they really *don't* value these things. I also have no problem with leaders interested in personal gain—unless they lie about it. If they say, "We're all in this together" but give themselves heavy raises, take credit for everything, try to build their résumé, and so on, that's not being honest. So, it's important for leaders to be self-aware. They need to understand and live values that support other people. Ultimately, we get when we give. —HOWARD BEHAR

One implication of being clear about our values is that we must also be true to ourselves. Leaders should avoid aligning with causes and organizations that violate their own dignity and the dignity of others about whom they care. And they need to be comfortable speaking up and expressing their own views, even when it may feel awkward or unpopular:

[E]arly in my career, I used to hold back if my opinion differed from the group. I thought it might be seen as too aggressive to express a different opinion. And you do need to fit into a culture. As an Asian American, I was brought up to have the humility to blend in, not stand out. Now, I see my integrity as more important. I know I have knowledge and experience that's relevant. So, I know it's important to speak my truth regardless of whether it goes against what others think.

I've also learned that there are different ways to say it—that how you say it matters. Humility helps with this. I'll indicate, "I don't need everyone to agree with me, but I see things a bit differently here. And I'll own that this is my view, but I want to express my concerns." So, it's important to own your truth and be confident about it, but not obnoxious. Sometimes you have to express your view two or three times to have it considered well. But you also have to be willing to listen, and to recognize that sometimes it's best to let go of your opinion. You won't always prevail, but it's important to express yourself. —PHYLLIS CAMPBELL

Finally, integrity requires taking responsibility and doing the right thing. Leaders are responsible for outcomes in their zone of influence, and they need to fully accept this. It is rarely appropriate for leaders to blame others when things go wrong. This damages others' dignity and shirks the leader's responsibility. When a leader blames others publicly, it is seen as scapegoating—protecting oneself by sacrificing others. Instead, leaders should take public responsibility—even if they later have a private conversation with those whose mistakes contributed to the problem. By publicly taking responsibility, leaders show support for those who worked with them even though mistakes were made. The dignity of others is supported (and loyalty to the leader often increases) because they were not embarrassed. By contrast, leaders should be careful not to take credit for work others have done, but respect others' dignity by giving credit to those who merit it. This can include public praise, if appropriate.

Organizational Impact

Balanced ego and robust integrity are important keys to leader humility because they signal to others who you are. These keys have a positive effect on many common functions that leaders perform. This section discusses the impact of ego and integrity on attracting and retaining talent, diversity and inclusion, performance management, teamwork and forging consensus on issues, and brand reputation.

Attracting and Retaining Talent

Leaders who are arrogant will have problems attracting talent if people know much about them. I once consulted with an organization whose CEO was highly regarded for his expertise, yet most people interacted with him stiffly (superficial smiles, little eye contact, minimal verbal exchange). The board's concern was that it had great difficulty attracting senior leadership talent in its field. Too often, the company was forced to make multiple offers at excessive compensation to get someone to accept. The CEO's peers and employees recognized that the problem was his conceit. Every conversation quickly became all about him. Not surprisingly, job candidates had discovered this too as word had gotten around professional circles, and many preferred not to work for him.

In a similar way, reputations are earned for a leader's integrity—or immoral behavior. Few people want to work for leaders whose personal conduct is poor. Most prefer to work for those they can respect and admire. Leaders who lack integrity lose, or lose the respect of, good employees.

Diversity and Inclusion

Because everyone's dignity is composed differently, people whose backgrounds differ from the norm (such as people of color and women) will often value aspects of their being that are not well represented or popular in the dominant culture. Having a balanced ego helps leaders avoid the pitfall of assuming that diverse team members are somehow less important. It can also help them learn how common stereotypes affect others so that, as leaders, they can avoid those stereotypes and better support the dignity of diverse stakeholders.

For example, leaders who are women and/or members of racial or cultural minority groups report specific challenges around how they are seen ("Who I Am"), much of which has been supported by research. A fairly common issue affecting female leaders is that people view the same behaviors differently, depending on who is exhibiting them:

> Three quarters of my leadership team is female, and we have this discussion often. We see that people have different perceptions of style. For example, people have different perceptions about humility or anger depending on who is showing it, even if the behavior is identical. My team will point out that if a man shows anger, he's seen as having a strong opinion, but if a woman does it, she's seen as too emotional or out of control. We are out of balance in how the same behavior is seen and judged for different groups. We stereotype African American men, women, etc. So, people in certain groups do have to think carefully about how they would come across to others using the same behavior. —ORLANDO ASHFORD

This comment speaks to the unfortunate reality that women face a more limited range of acceptable behavior before others judge them as too meek or too arrogant, so women find they have to walk a narrower path. This is also true for men who are racial minorities:

> I think there are different—and somewhat risky—challenges. There has to be a delicate balance of being

humble without appearing to be too diffident. You don't want to step back too far. There's a presumption with white males that they are confident. For African Americans and others, an important balance has to be struck so that humility doesn't come across as lacking in confidence. At the same time, you don't want to be viewed as too aggressive. —ROGER FERGUSON

And those raised with different cultural norms may find that assumptions about their behavior create leadership challenges. Leaders from culturally diverse backgrounds often find that they need to adapt their behaviors to fit majority-group expectations:

On a personal level, I also had to learn how not to be stereotypical. There's a meekness expected of Asian women. I've had some good coaches that helped with this. Once I was given an award, and one of them told me, "You were so humble, you looked at your shoes as if you were embarrassed to receive the award." This same person helped me understand that my behavior discounts the giver. I had to consider that. In my Japanese upbringing, I was taught that the nail that sticks up gets hammered down. I later realized that if someone is trying to honor you, you honor them by being a welcome recipient. So, you have to own your success too but without hubris. —PHYLLIS CAMPBELL

Finally, leaders who lack ego balance, particularly those who are arrogant, will tend to assume they know everything. They are less open to hearing different views—a behavior that particularly disadvantages those whose experience is most different (such as minorities and women). Arrogant leaders tend to perpetuate systems that are uncomfortable for diverse team members.

Performance Management

"Who I Am" has a lot to do with motivating people to engage and give their all. Leaders who are arrogant are seen as being all about themselves. It is hard for others to put full energy behind leaders who are self-serving. By contrast, when leaders have a balanced ego, they genuinely regard the dignity of others. Fear and intimidation are removed from the environment, and people are more inclined to offer their best efforts.

Integrity also contributes to better performance. When leaders behave with integrity, their communication is predictable and authentic. As others find they can trust their leader, they are more forthcoming with information. This includes surfacing problems so that they can be resolved early. This improves collaboration and performance.

Teamwork and Consensus

An essential element in the work of leadership is the need to influence people, whether individually or in groups. Heavy-handed use of power and expressions of arrogance are likely to be met with counterforce. It may be possible in the short run to dominate or win, but this is likely to cause backlash later—or stalemate in the interim. Consider situations like labor strikes or government shutdowns. These represent high-stakes, win-lose tactics that affect hundreds or thousands of people. They often involve loss of pay and unavailability of services. What people really want is progress, honest communication, and compromise for a better offer. These ultimately come when the confrontation is resolved, but at the cost of resentment and deepened mistrust. Win-lose tactics tend to inflame conflict rather than resolve it, because those who have been harmed remember how they were treated and are less inclined to work together well in the future.

Win-lose strategies also encourage expressions of extreme positions. These often include distortions of fact with an accompanying loss of trust and backlash. People have reasonable access to verifying what leaders say.

Brand Reputation

Organizations make many mistakes that prove embarrassing to their brand or reputation. Because public relations are important, it is natural for leaders to want to minimize exposure of problems or misdeeds. Yet, if facts are distorted, damage to reputation occurs, and it can be long-lasting. The integrity with which leaders handle communication makes a big difference in how quickly and effectively trust is restored following public relations crises.

> You can also look at the way businesses respond to crises.
> Humility has a BIG impact, and it affects public relations.
> Some leaders are defensive, but some will own their part
> of the problem. For example, in the mid-'90s when Nike
> was called out for using child labor, even though it was
> occurring through contractors in their supply chain,
> their reaction showed self-reflection and a willingness to
> change. That took humility. —SALLY JEWELL

Having looked at how the keys of balanced ego and robust integrity affect common leader functions, it's important to understand specific behaviors that support these keys. Table 2 provides a sample list of dos and don'ts regarding ego and integrity.

TABLE 2. "Who I Am": Recommended Behaviors.

BALANCED EGO	
DO	DON'T
Feel proud of yourself but show more curiosity about others' successes.	Boast about your own possessions, achievements, etc.
Indicate in word and action that others are important to you, even when criticizing their decisions or actions.	Be condescending or insulting to others.
Show confidence in handling responsibilities.	Regularly display meekness or lack of confidence.
Recognize and acknowledge that the work gets done through others.	Take credit for work that was shared by many.
Take personal responsibility for mistakes/responsibilities.	Blame others for your mistakes, or publicly blame them for mistakes they may have made.
Take responsibility for problems in the organization you lead.	See yourself as the center of the organization's success.
INTEGRITY	
DO	DON'T
Understand that values are seen through what you do, not what you say.	Act in ways that fail to support what you say you believe in.
Be true to your word.	Tell lies, stretch the truth, or distort information.
Adapt your behavior to be appropriate with cultural expectations while staying true to your ideas.	Allow your behavior to reinforce negative cultural stereotypes (such as about women or minorities), knowing that these do not characterize you.
Keep commitments and responsibilities, including follow-through on appointments and communication.	Ignore others' needs for your presence and time or share confidential information without permission.

> **IDEAS FOR ACTION**

Balanced Ego

1. Observe whether people are willing to criticize your recommendations or decisions. Ideally, they will be, because no one is perfect. Notice how you respond. Are you typically receptive or defensive?

2. Monitor how often you talk about yourself (interests, connections, achievements, etc.) in conversations with stakeholders compared with how often you inquire genuinely about others. Maintain a lesser or equal focus on yourself in discussions with others.

3. Do subordinates seem comfortable teasing you? Or do they seem intimidated and overly deferential? Comfort in teasing usually means your ego is not in the way of their relating to you.

Integrity

1. Do you generally keep appointments with stakeholders? Meet deadlines? Respond to email and calls? Deliver what you promise? These address implied or explicit commitments to others. Failing to respond as expected shows a lack of integrity in relating to others.

2. List the five to eight values that are most important to you in work and life. Using a 1 to 5 scale, with 5 meaning very strong and 1 meaning very weak, how would you rate your behavior on each (how you actually show up on them)? Since these values are most important to you, do you see areas where you need to adjust your behavior to match your beliefs about what you value?

3. Do you feel you can communicate the same accurate information to all your stakeholders? Or do you think you need to modify it for different audiences? How do you share information if/when your organization discovers big mistakes? What guides your answers to these questions? Are there ways to improve *alignment* in your messaging?

CHAPTER FIVE

The Direction I Set

Leadership is the capacity to translate vision into reality.
—Warren Bennis

Establishing compelling vision and ethical strategies are keys to supporting others' dignity, as shown in figure 7. You might be wondering, "How on earth is setting direction related to humility? Isn't it up to the leader to determine the best vision and strategy to achieve what's desired?" The answer becomes evident when we remember that leaders *need people*—let's call them followers—to embrace and implement the proposed direction. And leaders have to convert many types of stakeholders into followers, whether peers, customers, employees, suppliers, legislators, or community citizens. Because so many

FIGURE 7. Keys to "The Direction I Set."

others typically need to buy into a planned direction, the days of the lone-wolf leader are over. Setting direction without engaging stakeholders and addressing their concerns is a recipe for failed implementation.

People want to feel proud of both the work they do and the cause(s) they serve, so vision needs to support the larger common good. People also want to know that the way their organizations operate is ethical. These wants reflect deep values—how people see themselves and what makes them feel worthy. In other words, what they want is keenly tied to their dignity. So, leaders need humility to consider others' dignity, establish a vision serving all stakeholders, and then create strategies (and measures of progress) to implement that vision. Consider just a few examples of how others' dignity is relevant to vision and strategies:

- Many employees, particularly younger ones, seek employers whose visions contribute public benefit. They are often sensitive to the impact of business operations on climate change and social good. Their sense of dignity influences how they choose to spend their talents and energies. Leaders with humility show regard for this trend by setting positive visions.

- Since the publication of the UN Environment Programme's (Knoepfel 2004) landmark report "Who Cares Wins," investor attention has extended to organizations' focus on environmental, social, and governance (ESG) factors because these factors influence risk and future financial returns. Many people's values align with favorable ESG activities, and their dignity is offended by visions that harm others or the environment. Investopedia (2019) reported that $11.6 trillion was invested in ESG incorporation assets. CEOs also recognize the importance of visions that support ESG. A statement by the Business Roundtable (2019) was signed by 181 CEOs affirming that shareholder wealth is no longer the sole purpose of businesses; broader stakeholder interests must be considered.

• In the technology sector, the *Observer* (Bonzanno 2018) reported that employees at Google pressed it to withdraw from competing for Pentagon contracts because employees protested against making profits from defense contracts. The *Los Angeles Times* (Peltz 2019) described how Amazon employees have pressured the company to address environmental issues. And Reuters (Hunnicutt 2019) reported how Twitter and Facebook responded to pressure from stakeholders to take responsibility for allowing their platforms to be used to spread false information in political ads. Stakeholders' dignity was negatively affected by their leaders' approach to generating revenue when the directions were seen as harmful to others. Leaders with humility have begun to respond to these challenges and consider alternative strategies.

The work of some companies is widely viewed as harmful (for example, tobacco companies), as are the strategies of others (such as Purdue Pharma, accused of practices that excessively pushed prescriptions and contributed to the epidemic of opioid addiction). It is difficult, if not impossible, to turn a blind eye to these types of harmful visions and strategies—or to frame them in truly positive ways. But for many leaders (if not most), the challenge is thinking more broadly—and humbly—about human dignity. What is it we do—or what can we do—that has a positive impact on the larger common good? Setting a compelling vision is one of the most important keys to leader humility. When coupled with ethical strategies, it has a positive effect on others' dignity and generates favorable results. Let's look at both of these keys to humility more closely.

Compelling Vision

The CEOs I interviewed stressed that vision is compelling when it serves a *greater good*. The vision must be much broader than the leader's proximate responsibility or personal interests. Although business leaders are rightfully concerned with competitive advantage and profitability, employees and customers typically have other concerns or priorities. Here is an excellent example of how an operating vision is framed in terms of the greater good:

> To get an organization to a certain scale, people have
> to work for the organization and not just the leader. . . .
> [M]ost of us don't want to come to work to fulfill some-
> one else's vision . . . we want to feel like we're accom-
> plishing a higher purpose. I think our employees know
> that what we're doing isn't about Brad's vision. It's about
> Alaska being the best company that we can possibly
> be—connecting families and communities, and helping

businesses grow, while providing excellent jobs for our folks. —BRAD TILDEN

Tilden's humility is evident in expressing his vision in a compelling way and noting that it is not about him personally. By framing the vision in terms of "connecting families and communities," and so on, he elevates the work being done so that employees and customers see the larger impact. "Helping businesses grow" shows the positive impact on suppliers, and "providing excellent jobs" not only appeals to employee dignity but supports favorable brand reputation (compared with companies that are viewed as treating employees poorly). Importantly, each of these elements supports the dignity of others in a compelling way.

Vision also needs to be relevant to many stakeholders, not merely shareholders. Some aspects of compelling vision may be embedded in an organization's core operation (as in the example above). Another way of enhancing the core vision is through decisions that affect the greater good directly—while indirectly affecting the organization in a positive way. JPMorgan Chase provides a good illustration:

> There's a whole ecosystem of stakeholders. This includes the communities in which we operate. So, it takes enlightened self-interest and humility to see that and act on it. Because we derive our business from the community, it's important for the community to be strong. We want the underserved parts of the community to be strong too. That's why we invested $200 million plus in Detroit. A community is not a healthy community unless all parts are strong. Some of the risks of

community weakness include theft, violence, and small business bankruptcies. So, risk mitigation is part of the motivation for us, but it's also our ethos because it's the right thing to do. We are about building long-term relationships. We look at the whole causal loop. And we take that all the way through our culture and incentives. —PHYLLIS CAMPBELL

In addition to a positive core operation or supplemental efforts that enhance a vision, service to others (that is, servant leadership) can make visions inspirational and compelling. An emphasis on understanding clients, empathizing with their needs, and placing their interests first can motivate teams because many people's dignity is enhanced by providing service to others. Consider this perspective from a financial organization whose CEO explained to me that he doesn't "get a second chance to take good care of people's life savings" (that is, manage their retirement accounts successfully):

I think of myself as the *steward* of TIAA while I lead it. We are not publicly traded, yet we are a 100-year-old company with a trillion dollars in assets. Empathy for others is consistent with our mission. We are driven to identify with the people we serve. So being humble in how we think of our clients and in how we serve them is just part of who we are. —ROGER FERGUSON

Stewardship, of course, can extend beyond the immediate organization and its clients, and even beyond the present. We lead in ways that can affect the larger commons—the environment, communities around us, and even future generations. Leader humility can extend deep regard not only for other people but also

for the natural world when we consider potential impact
broadly:

> Seeing ourselves in context is an important attribute. . . .
> Overseeing the Department of the Interior was the most
> challenging job I've ever held, with the potential to impact
> many people and the environment. It was also a position
> where there were powerful influences working to shape
> decisions that served particular interests. The most difficult
> decisions I had to make were shaped by thinking about
> the impact on future generations, guided by my favorite
> proverb, "We don't inherit the earth from our ancestors, we
> borrow it from our children." . . . Humility in leadership is
> needed whenever the human stands in relation to the envi-
> ronment. —SALLY JEWELL

It can be hard for one person, the leader alone, to
determine the best and most compelling vision. Leaders
may need to reach deep and wide into the organization
or broader stakeholder groups to form an appropriate
and compelling vision. And, as leaders solicit broader
views, it is equally important for them to really listen.
Some leaders pay lip service to wanting input but quickly
ignore ideas or concerns that are difficult to address or
might pull them off their original path. Deep listening is
evident when leaders incorporate the information gained
into the overall vision, as described in the following
examples:

> In 2005, when I became CEO, a top priority was to make
> REI a much more sustainable company. One of my col-
> leagues sought expertise from the outside to facilitate
> a gathering with about two dozen employees in posi-
> tions from across REI to help map out our impact on

the biosphere. These employees provided a variety of insights into our practices that were revealing, and in some cases disturbing, yet helped us create a road map for the future. They helped us understand where to find "the low-hanging fruit" and how we could have the biggest positive impact. We hired an expert in sustainability and continued to reach out deep into the organization to improve our practices and use our influence to shape the practices of our vendors. These stories get out, and they create an environment where people are more willing to speak up.

At Interior . . . I had many handlers trying to control my time. Early on, they'd schedule a visit to a park, facility, or tribe for me to have a fast meeting, then race to another site, grabbing a sandwich on the way. I said, "Whoa! I'm not leaving without spending time to meet the people who carry out our work to better understand their jobs and how we can support their mission." For example, on public lands, I wanted to meet with rangers, firefighters, scientists, people on the frontlines and behind the scenes, to better understand our responsibilities. With tribes, I learned the importance of showing respect, which included allowing time to get to know them personally and see firsthand their cultures and better understand my role in carrying out our government-to-government responsibilities. —SALLY JEWELL

Because this approach can generate more effective visions, it is especially important for situations in which there are conflicting goals or when different stakeholder groups have competing interests. But it's also true when dealing with innovation and complex problems like sustainability.

Creating compelling vision is a key behavior in leader humility because it regards the dignity of others. Many stakeholders will be affected by the direction you set, so a tepid vision will not generate much enthusiasm. A vision that's all about you will generate even less. And a harmful vision will invite strong resistance. Instead, a vision that preserves, protects, or improves a greater good *inspires* people to participate—because the work has more meaning to them. Their sense of dignity is enhanced by the association.

Ethical Strategies

Strategies are designed as the best paths to desired outcomes, but some leaders engage in unethical practices. There are news reports of leadership misdeeds almost daily; these negatively affect the dignity of stakeholders who feel tainted by association. The sheer frequency of misdeeds has contributed to a broadly jaded and negative view of leadership in both public and private sectors. Leaders who pursue unethical approaches display a significant lack of regard for the dignity of others.

Ethical strategies can be developed by carefully understanding business opportunities and aligning others to pursue those approaches. Leaders who do this respect others' dignity. Some of the best strategies used by humble leaders involve competitive pricing, fair employee compensation, collaboration and integration of operations to minimize waste, and alignment of direction across the organization in ethical pursuit of business opportunity. The following two cases illustrate how this can work quite well.

Costco is a stellar example. It achieved the exceptional size it is today (approximately 254,000 employees across forty-four states, thirteen countries, and nearly eight hundred warehouse retail locations) largely without paid advertising, although it has received much favorable media attention. Instead of media advertising, Costco relied on membership renewals and a fair profit from sales. Its code of conduct, merchandising, and treatment of employees all reflect an ethical strategy of providing excellent value to customers and employees, thus respecting their dignity:

> We always set a fair markup and never simply raise it just because we can. We don't believe in hype—just put the product out there with a basic description and let people decide for themselves. We've always sought to offer the best wages and best benefits in the industry.
> —JIM SINEGAL

Note that paying good wages and benefits is strategic: it helps with employee retention and engagement. It also demonstrates leader humility by supporting the dignity of others. Another company known for this in the retail industry is Starbucks, which became a trailblazer years ago by providing employment benefits (such as health insurance) to part-time workers. Beyond its progressive compensation, it also developed an ethical approach that centered on the customer experience:

> Starbucks is a people-centric business. Our baristas interface directly with a lot of people. So, our business is about relationships—meaning trust and caring. That's how we grew the business. I used to have a sign in my office that

said, "We are in the people business serving coffee, not the coffee business serving people." —HOWARD BEHAR

This focus was powerful strategically because it generated a qualitatively different customer experience. As evidence of its effectiveness, Starbucks had just twenty-eight stores when Behar joined the firm in 1989; his leadership helped it become a global giant before his retirement in 2007.

As with technology and manufacturing, customer-focused models can involve significant complexity. When they do, collaboration and integration of operations need to be an integral part of the strategy. The Mayo Clinic, widely known and respected in the health care sector, is a good example of how collaboration and integration can be baked into strategic direction. Mayo requires humility from all team members to support patients' health and dignity:

Patients come to the Mayo Clinic for one of two reasons: One, they may have a very serious illness with a known diagnosis, but nothing so far has resolved it. We may be the best and last hope they have of healing. Or two, they come to us because they have a serious, complex, and puzzling set of symptoms, but "no one knows what's wrong with me." In both cases, it takes a team of care providers collaborating to help the patient.

So, our approach is interdisciplinary. A given case may involve a cardiologist, an endocrinologist, a pulmonologist, a hematologist, a nutritionist, a physical therapist, and so on. Each of them will be highly accomplished as individuals, and they need to have the humility to work together to help the patient. Figuratively, they will have to sit around the dining room table and put their heads together to figure out how to help the patient within two to three hours. Also, nearly 20 percent of our surgeries are done by teams of surgeons (for example, thoracic, vascular, and cardiology surgeons).

We measure a wide range of outcomes. Patient outcomes are essential: We care about outcomes such as safety and quality, adverse events. We also care about the academic performance of our associates. In addition, we measure business outcomes, such as fundraising, brand management, financial performance, business development, endowment (funding research efforts, start-up companies, etc.). We are in the top decile of performance on each measure, and our staff retention is excellent. Our turnover is only 2 percent of staff and scientists. Success in each of these comes from our culture of teams and individuals working together. —JOHN NOSEWORTHY, MD

A final aspect of strategy needs to be mentioned: organizational alignment. Leaders often think they need to preserve confidentiality of plans and financial information. This may be the case if intellectual property is at stake. But some leaders hold information closely because it reinforces their sense of status. By contrast, humble leaders find strategic advantage in disseminating information to all stakeholders so that everyone engaged in the work understands the goals and status. This not only improves focus but supports ethical behavior when goals and processes are publicly disclosed:

If our entire organization is not aligned behind the same purpose, we have no chance to get there. It takes humility to realize you can't do it by yourself. That's

why we are open and transparent. Our website is very
clear about our strategies and financials, so everyone
in the company has the information. People know
they are included. We all have a constancy of purpose.

—DICK JOHNSON

Organizational Impact

Compelling vision and ethical strategies have significant impact on leader effectiveness. They not only set
direction but affect the extent to which leaders get stakeholders to follow planned directions. Some areas that are
commonly affected by vision and strategies are talent
management; brand reputation; diversity and inclusion;
and performance management, teamwork, and consensus building.

Attracting and Retaining Talent

Finding and keeping great talent is important regardless of whether the economy is strong or weak. Having
a compelling vision and ethical strategies matters to
many workers, especially those who are educated and
affluent because they often have multiple opportunities,
and they scrutinize leader behavior and impact. Organizations with compelling visions are more attractive
to them than those whose visions are uninspiring—or
worse, known to be harmful to people or the environment. When strategies and practices are seen as being
ethical, an organization's desirability as a place to work
or do business increases. Consider how, in the consumer
world, online ratings have come into use for products,
services, and professional providers like doctors, lawyers,
and professors. Just as user ratings of their experiences

now guide others' purchase decisions, reputation for ethics and compelling vision guide employment choices.

In a similar way, many younger employees tend to seek association with inspiring causes. They have a high sense of self-worth (dignity) and want to see their energies being used positively. Leaders who set compelling visions and gain reputations for ethical strategies have an advantage in attracting and keeping younger talent.

Brand Reputation

Vision and strategy affect external reputation, sometimes positively and sometimes less so. Consider the 2018 incident in which two African American men were arrested for merely sitting in a Starbucks in Philadelphia (Tornoe 2018). The immediate outcry from the public and the African American community forced the company's leadership to respond. Recognizing both the unfairness of the incident and the diversity of its customer base, the company's leadership opted for a strategy that emphasized its ethical behavior. The CEO, Kevin Johnson, called the incident a "reprehensible outcome." He publicly released a letter (Johnson 2018) apologizing to the two men, asserting that the company stood against discrimination and racial profiling, and stating that the company would investigate what happened and make changes to its practices to help ensure that it didn't happen again. The company, in fact, closed its stores for a day to provide training on implicit bias. Johnson's note told employees and customers that they had the right to expect more from Starbucks and promised to learn from the incident and improve. NPR (2018) reported that the company closed roughly eight thousand stores on May

29, 2018, to provide racial-bias training to approximately 175,000 employees. This involved significant expense, as well as lost revenue.

Was this mainly spin or public relations? I think it was more than that. It goes to the heart of leader humility as sound strategy. Understanding the dignity of both the employees who work for the company and the customers who provide its revenue, Starbucks embraces diversity and inclusion strategically. A tepid response would have led to broad and ongoing criticism, so certainly one goal was damage control. However, the company's moves to meet with the gentlemen who had been arrested, issue a public apology in which the leaders owned their mistakes, close stores (losing significant revenue), and provide corrective training to 175,000 employees were very strong statements that the company was serious about this. Because the strategic response so clearly displayed regard for the dignity of others (the men arrested, the African American community, employees who were embarrassed by the incident, etc.), it showed humility. In turn, sales were not hurt significantly by the demonstrations, and the negative press was reduced significantly and quickly. Although this helped with PR, it clearly showed both the vision and strategy the company's leaders wanted to pursue.

Diversity and Inclusion

Because everyone's dignity is important, leaders with humility also consider multiple groups when setting vision and strategy. The following questions highlight relevant considerations:

1. Are we including the views of diverse groups in discussions and decisions about our vision and strategies? The best way to learn about and be able to anticipate their needs is to engage with them. The process of engaging them often will increase their buy-in to an eventual decision.

2. Do we consider the impact on their communities as we learn about that? And do we adjust our vision/strategy to try seriously to balance their needs with those of others?

3. Does our employment reasonably reflect, our customer or user base so that we have people who can advise us of their needs? Do we listen?

4. Is there diversity on our board of directors so that our vision and strategies are vetted through a powerful lens that reflects broader views?

5. Do we view diversity and inclusion as an asset in the ways we do business? Consider Nike's strategy of featuring football's renowned Colin Kaepernick in an ad for its products despite the ongoing controversy surrounding his taking a knee during the US national anthem. *Fast Company* (Beer 2019) reported that, despite doomsday predictions by some, Nike gained significantly by taking a supportive stance on Kaepernick, thus against biased policing. Nike understood that their consumer base is diverse.

Performance Management, Teamwork, and Consensus

When leaders with humility use the keys of vision and strategy appropriately, others identify with the vision because it supports their sense of dignity, or self-worth. This tends to draw out their best efforts, which means better performance.

Because of the complexity of work, collaboration is often required. This might be across departments in an organization or across the aisle at every level of government. It may also be with community partnerships or regulatory enforcement. When leaders have humility to consider the dignity of all parties to the collaboration— and when leaders support others' dignity—they secure support more readily. This usually requires identifying overarching goals, shared values for a win-win, and elements that may need compromise. However, progress is more likely (and more likely to be sustained) in this way than with a winner-take-all approach. Compelling visions and ethical strategies reasonably honor all affected parties, thereby providing easier buy-in.

Having examined areas in which compelling vision and ethical strategies typically affect leader outcomes, let's again look at specific behaviors that are positive or negative. Table 3 illustrates dos and don'ts that leaders should consider. This is followed by suggested ideas for action.

TABLE 3. "The Direction I Set": Recommended Behaviors.

COMPELLING VISION	
DO	**DON'T**
Create a vision that serves a noble purpose.	Make it mainly about you.
Advance products, services, and ideas that enhance the broader social good.	Violate the social good by offering damaging goods and services just to make a profit, win an election, or secure personal benefit.
Consider potential negative impact on different groups of people. Include diversity in your deliberations.	Ignore the needs and concerns of other groups because you can dominate.
Anticipate and minimize environmental impact.	Overlook responsibility for climate change.
Seek to provide gains for all partners and stakeholders.	Limit your focus to shareholder gains.
ETHICAL STRATEGIES	
DO	**DON'T**
Obey the law.	Do what is illegal.
Be fair to all stakeholders.	Do what is unfair or shady to secure goals.
Model strong values and ethics.	Be secretive and underhanded.
Make sure that partners behave in ethical ways.	Allow partners or those who represent you to use unethical means to support your goals.

IDEAS FOR ACTION

Compelling Vision

1. In what ways does your work help people? Does it somehow serve a greater good? Are there any harmful side effects? As a leader, think through the strongest impact of your work.

2. What is your stance toward skeptics and naysayers? Do you exclude them and go your own way? If so, consider inviting them to work with you. How might they help you achieve a better outcome?

3. Can you frame your vision inspirationally? Try to create a shared goal that diverse stakeholders can unite in wanting to support. What is the most positive—yet honest— message you can share with others about the vision you pursue?

Ethical Strategies

1. Have you seen competitive practices that you believe are wrong but that others use in order to get ahead? Do you follow along? Where do you draw your own line?

2. Are you willing (and able) to speak up if you see unethical behavior in your organization?

3. Identify three ways you can model ethical strategies. Would it help to discuss these with stakeholders to ensure your (and their) accountability?

CHAPTER SIX

How I Treat You

*Train people well enough so they can leave. Treat
them well enough so they don't want to.*

—Richard Branson

"Do You See Me?" is perhaps the most critical question
people have when asked to work with a leader. It implies:
Do I matter to you? Do you understand my views and my
needs? Am I merely a pawn for you to use in achieving
your goals, or do you care about me as a person with my
own thoughts and needs? Do you get my potential as a
partner in this work? And are you willing to work with
me even though we will not always see eye to eye?

People look closely at how leaders treat them in answering these questions for themselves. So, the final two keys
to supporting others' dignity address leader behaviors
that show others that they are seen. As shown in figure
8, one of the biggest tipoffs is how generous you are with
inclusion: whether and how you involve others in discussions and decisions—and of what importance. The other
type of behavior that people will notice is your focus
on their broader development. Do you seem concerned

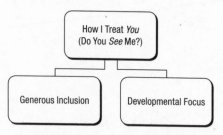

FIGURE 8. Keys to "How I Treat You."

only that they do what you ask today? Or do you show that you are cultivating a relationship with them for the longer term by helping them grow professionally? Let's consider generous inclusion and developmental focus in turn.

Generous Inclusion

A common mistake among leaders is assuming they are supposed to know most everything—that their high status means others have little to contribute to their work. Some assume they know what's best for others, even when they are aware that some parties who will be affected by decisions hold different opinions. Rather than facilitate discussions to surface and resolve differing views, many leaders make decisions without involving others and later try to sell the decision or frame it as being in others' best interest.

Have you noticed problems with this approach? It frequently fails because implementation goes awry. And that often happens when leaders lack adequate information, misjudge others' real needs, or damage others' dignity by signaling that they are not important enough to consult. People who are close to the action—in the trenches, so to speak—know when and how their own insights can make a difference. Although they have different roles, they often have significant knowledge, motivation, skill, and connections to advance the work at hand. Overlooking this fact signals that leaders are not seeing them.

> I believe what William Worrall Mayo said: "No one is big enough to be independent of others." We need to have a union of forces. That's even more true today when the explosion of knowledge is such that none of us can know everything. Humility is needed to lead and work with others. If we really want to be successful, let's get together and figure out how everybody's gifts can contribute. —JOHN NOSEWORTHY, MD

Although command-and-control methods may yield compliance, generous inclusion makes partners in your work feel seen and valued. At its simplest, *inclusion means inviting people to be part of the real action.* Inclusion goes far beyond calling people together for staff meetings that simply provide face time, share routine reports, or delegate to others work you don't want to do. Rarely do those actions result in people feeling seen, with the possible exception of the initial invitations to meet. Instead, generous inclusion requires thinking about whom you are engaging, on what activities, and in what way.

- **Who should be included:** It is especially important to involve people who are likely to have a strong, negative emotional response to your choices or the direction you set. Decisions that affect others (such as work, status, pay, or any detriment to well-being) call for generous inclusion. This applies not only to employees but to peers, members of your supply chain or community—anyone who is likely to be affected significantly by what you are doing.

- **On what activities:** Generous inclusion means bringing others into discussions around *important* issues, such as significant business concerns, planning for future initiatives, resolving serious challenges, or generating quality improvements. It is when people are left out of important considerations that they feel they were not included, were not seen, did not matter.

- **In what way:** Inclusion needs to be authentic. It does not necessarily require delegating the final decision to a group, but it means sharing the issues and giving people voice, even when letting them know that their views will be advisory but not decisive. However, people do monitor how often you include their ideas in the final decision. Inclusion carries the expectation that you are really listening and care about others' dignity. Repeatedly asking for but discounting their input will be noticed, and you will be seen as lacking integrity and not being very inclusive.

To show genuine interest in others' ideas and opinions, we need to really listen, something many action-oriented leaders fail to do. When mindshare is divided between the person in front of us and other tasks or concerns, listening is compromised, and people sense our distraction. Genuine listening begins with devoted attention. And once our attention is focused only on the conversation at hand, it is important to stay open to what we are hearing. What usually happens instead is that we hear part of the input and immediately shift to planning our response. One tip is to listen as if we will hear something we can reinforce and act on favorably—to listen with positive expectation—and watch how others respond to this quality of attention.

> As a society, we have become enamored with the first sound bite we hear. People don't take time to listen to learn. They just listen to respond. An important part of humility in a leader is the ability to listen—to cast yourself in others' shoes. A humble leader . . . allows for free-form dialogue and for opinions to be offered as options. People are more engaged. —DICK JOHNSON

Of course, listening can occur only when others speak up. Sometimes people need encouragement to speak when you begin trying to include them. If employees or other partners in your work have been given little chance to contribute before, they may hesitate to offer their views. Instead, they may defer to your authority or assume that you simply want to issue direction.

I have heard leaders say, "I try to hold discussions, but no one really contributes anything." Leaders need to remain aware of their own power position—that others see their title and status and will likely defer to them unless given permission otherwise. If participation of others is lagging, it can help to clarify your intention. Consider this insight:

> As CEO, you're not entitled to an opinion or to express it. [*Smiles*] If you say one thing, the conversation is over. People think, "That's what Jeff thinks, so let's do

it." Often, I will just stay silent so the discussion can continue. This has been a real learning experience for me—seeing how whatever I say tends to be taken as direction when I don't mean it that way. So, if I want to offer an opinion, I usually preface it with, "Hey, I'm just one person in the room—just part of the discussion, so this is only an idea . . . " I've learned that there is a real difference between when you are just a seat at the table and when you are the CEO, and how sensitive people are to that position. —JEFF MUSSER

Not only is listening important; so is emotional generosity. This can involve the type of active signaling that Musser used to indicate a real desire for input. And it can be shown in passive ways, such as being patient while people formulate their own thoughts and not finishing sentences for them or filling the temporary silence with your own ideas. It may also involve prodding some stakeholders until they come around. This is particularly important when employees have significantly less power. It takes (and shows) emotional generosity to hold back so that others can thrive. Although that may be more time-consuming at first than simply being directive, in the long run, it creates a better container for working together:

Humility in leadership is most effective around the employee experience. It helps people do their best work for the company. I've learned that the most effective way to lead is through influence and not power. An example of that comes from parenting: toilet training is all influence and no power! And I once had a boss who told me, "You synthesize fast. You often get to the right answer quickly. The problem is you just say it. . . . Instead, why not ask questions? Nudge a little bit until they suggest it." The humility involved in doing that allows other people to contribute more. A humble leader creates a work environment where people feel more appreciated and valued. That translates into how they care for the customers, which then translates to revenue and profitability. —SALLY JEWELL

And while listening and emotional generosity are important to inclusion, they can be harder to provide when people's views are very different. I have heard seasoned managers complain about how younger employees have different expectations about work. I've seen leaders intentionally exclude from discussions people whose "backgrounds are different so they wouldn't understand." And I've known leaders who exclude key stakeholders from planning sessions because it takes too long to reach consensus when people assert different perspectives.

Sometimes, the leader's real desire is to advance his or her own agenda. It is tempting to believe we can achieve a better outcome without the interference of conflicting views. However, excluding people who have a genuine stake in the outcome will risk problems in implementation. People will not feel seen unless leaders have the humility to listen and integrate stakeholder views, even when those views *are* different.

I'm the son of an immigrant, so I realize that there, but for the grace of God, go I. Our economic growth is because we brought people into this country. Diversity brings different thinking into an organization. People bring different life experiences that help us in lots of ways. But we have to listen to people whose backgrounds are different. And it takes humility to listen. —HOWARD BEHAR

So, generous inclusion requires a positive attitude toward diversity (for example, national origin, gender, race, ability, sexual orientation). Are you genuinely open to those who come from a different background and have a different perspective? Or do you tend to judge them as inappropriate? Do you commonly default to including mainly people who share your own background because discussions with them feel easier and more comfortable? It takes effort to develop good representation of differences in organizations, but it takes equal attention to whether these different voices and views are actually heard in discussions and integrated into decisions.

Leaders who display generous inclusion are welcoming in their demeanor and, at times, make specific efforts to draw out and fully process the views of different others. Because humble leaders tend to feel (as well as display) regard for others' dignity, the emotionally welcoming stance is observed in the leader's body language and tone of voice, as well as in word.

> Humility is a foundation for supporting diversity. If you're humble, you know you don't have a monopoly on wisdom . . . that people with different life experiences will bring different points of view that will enrich what you're doing. That's why diversity is an advantage in an organization. But we can't just bring diverse people together; we have to be inclusive so that people feel valued, respected, and treated fairly—and so that we really hear their views and give them an opportunity to contribute their full potential. . . . There are many ways to engage others. For example, I prefer not to sit at the head of the table at meetings. I like to sit around the table, because I believe it sets a tone that invites the

others around the table to share their perspectives. The people I have admired most in life have been great at drawing other people in. —ROGER FERGUSON

Developmental Focus

Consider the difference between securing an Airbnb for a vacation, a year's lease on an apartment, and a mortgage on a home. All involve places to rest, but they mean different things and entail different levels of investment. The first two are largely transactional: they reflect short- and moderate-term commitments. When we sign up for them, we take little responsibility for caring for them beyond doing no harm. We generally care more about the apartment than the Airbnb because we're going to call it home for a while, but we are still unconcerned with its distant future. Yet buying a home is different: suddenly, repairs are our problem, and we start thinking about improvements and preventive maintenance.

A similar dynamic applies to how leaders think of partners at work. Which ones do you regard as fairly short-term transactions? Which as moderate-term? And which as long-term? Consider your bosses, peers, and employees, as well as those in your extended network, such as suppliers, customers, and the communities in which you reside. Let me suggest that the way you cultivate your relationships should have a developmental focus if you want others to feel seen.

Developmental focus implies *long-term* thinking. You care about the whole person and his or her progress beyond what is merely useful to you. For work partnerships like peers, suppliers, etc., you might show developmental focus by helping them understand your work, introducing them to helpful people in your network, and supporting their needs on occasion when it goes beyond the call of duty.

For those who report to you, developmental focus takes on deeper meaning. The power you hold can be used to support others' growth, neglect it, or sabotage it—and they are aware of this. Your role as leader can and should involve helping them learn in many ways, such as understanding the values of your specific organizational culture, how to do their job better, how to improve their knowledge of the context in which you operate so they have a better chance to advance, and how to manage others. Consider this compelling view:

> Culture isn't one person—it's omnipresent. You create
> that. I've said in the past that management is teach-
> ing. When we promote someone to management, I tell
> them that teaching is 90 percent of the job. If you just
> hire people and don't teach them, it's such a waste.
> And teaching isn't always formal. Do the right thing.
> Create a culture of doing the right thing—and you can't
> exempt yourself from this. I learned so much from my
> mentor Sol [Price]—that's where I got the importance of
> teaching. —JIM SINEGAL

As mentioned earlier, people in leadership often feel they have to know all the answers when this is not true. This is a common stumbling block for new managers who are often selected because they were outstanding individual contributors. They earned that recognition (and later promotion) by being expert at what they did—and carry into their new leadership role the desire to hold and display dominant expertise. This leads to overwhelm because the new leader's responsibilities have grown, and the desire to remain the expert interferes with delegating and developing others. Unfortunately, this tendency exists in some senior leaders, who continue to micromanage their teams. People who work below them know they can't take initiative without permission or make even small decisions without thorough review and approval. I have seen a team paralyzed in preparing for a company picnic because their senior executive insisted on reviewing everything—down to the color of the paper napkins.

In developing others, it's very important to recognize that some decisions really can be left to others. The outcome may differ from our personal preference, but . . . so what? Other situations may require oversight, but often the team can be given parameters for its decision that ensure it will be effective. Finally, leaders can delegate significantly by providing broad context and parameters, asking the team to allow the leader to have final approval, yet supporting the team's recommendations much of the time.

It is only by stretching that we grow. And leaders can develop others by posing relevant questions for their teams:

> As a leader, you don't have to know all the answers, but you do need to know all the questions. What if you just hold a key question for your team and then have confidence and trust in the team to solve it? You can let the discussion surface the issues that need to be handled, and all will then be invested in the outcome. —JIM WEBER

Another way in which leaders teach and show developmental focus is to place reasonable responsibility on their teams. This should involve *stretch* assignments, so that they are challenged to grow. In so doing, team member skills become stronger. It requires the leader to hold back on direction a bit, but it enables others to grow and feel pride in their accomplishments.

> Generally, I believe in stepping back and letting others learn and make decisions. I can think of some recent strategic decisions TIAA made. While I've set the strategic direction for where we should be going, I've left most of the negotiating decisions and choices about the specifics to my colleagues. Part of humility involves empowering your team to act. They should get to own and take pride in the outcomes. —ROGER FERGUSON

Organizational Impact

Having discussed how generous inclusion and developmental focus are keys to leader humility, let's now look at their impact on leader activities. These keys commonly influence a leader's effectiveness with talent management, diversity and inclusion, brand reputation, performance management, and teamwork and consensus building.

Attracting and Retaining Talent

"Do You See Me?" is especially important for these two aspects of talent management. People are less likely to take a job when, during the interview, they perceive that the environment is noninclusive. The more educated people are and the younger they are, the more they tend to want to be included in decisions and have their views heard. Prospective employees will be sensitive to cues about inclusion during interviews, not only related to them personally, but also about whether organizational leaders seek or limit input from a wide range of stakeholders.

Younger employees also care about long-term opportunities. They may ask about advancement possibilities, travel options, or the chance to gain multiple skills. They'll listen not only for information on growth options but also for signals that the organization and its leaders are willing to invest in their growth beyond the immediate job vacancy.

Inclusion and developmental focus are also very important when it comes to retaining employees. Lacking inclusion, employees can grow frustrated enough to leave. They know that they can contribute more and deserve greater appreciation. A lack of developmental focus suggests that their leaders think of them in a transactional way—meaning that leaders view employees as being just here, for now, to do a job. In response, the best and brightest employees are the ones most likely to leave. Leaders show that employees are seen by demonstrating interest in their development and providing support for future opportunities.

Some leaders hesitate to develop employees because they fear the employees will move to another job and the leader will have to rehire and retrain. Although this is a legitimate concern, it focuses on the leader's interests. It neglects what may be best for the employee who has a larger set of concerns and goals. And it hurts the organization, which benefits most when employees are developed to their full potential.

Diversity and Inclusion and Brand Reputation

Diversity presents both challenges and opportunities to leaders when trying to involve different voices in discussions. Yet diversity and inclusion are especially important in customer-facing businesses. Customers assess whether they are represented in what they see in your employees and practices, and it can affect how they view your brand. For retail- and service-oriented businesses, customers can readily see how diverse your employee base appears when they visit your business. They will judge for themselves whether you appear to make reasonable efforts to reflect your customer base. But customers will also gauge the happiness of diverse employees as an indicator of how well they are treated. Finally, they will consider whether the organization's products and policies are a good match for them. This may be seen in its advertising, its community focus, and the tailoring of its products for diverse audiences.

Importantly, being inclusive is not all about other people but also about the leader's own self-awareness. Sometimes, subtle conversational signals are taken in ways that were unintended. However, it is the leader's responsibility to self-reflect and ask if his or her own behavior should change. Leaders may need training in implicit bias to understand how they react to others when it comes to diversity and inclusion. As seen in the example mentioned earlier of the incident at Starbucks in Philadelphia, diversity and inclusion hold significant implications for brand reputation. Having a developmental focus on this topic with all employees is essential.

Performance Management

Generous inclusion and developmental focus enhance performance. Inclusion helps because people gain a broad understanding of organizational issues, along with specific knowledge they might not otherwise have. It also helps because they learn more about the organization's values and how its leaders must integrate multiple factors into decisions. When people hold a broad understanding of the organization and its goals as a result of inclusion, they have a context for what they are doing that tends to increase both their motivation and their performance.

Developmental focus improves the long game. Employees are more motivated to perform for leaders who hold much more than a transactional view of employment. And when employees are supported in developing to their full potential, they can contribute more to the organization.

Teamwork and Consensus

Inclusion is most challenging when people hold views that may be unfamiliar to us or counter to what we'd like to hear. However, so many of the challenges we face require that we collaborate and reach consensus. Seeking consensus is different than dominating to win or seeking majority approval. Consensus is achieved when all parties think the agreement is at least reasonably acceptable to them.

Blending different voices in rigorous discussion is a challenge because they will tend to push and pull each other. It requires a great deal of listening—sometimes very deep listening—to try to appreciate others' experiences and views. It is also likely to require compromise.

Rigorous discussion, deep listening, and compromise all take humility. But it is only through this generous inclusion that we can understand and forge consensus.

Let's now consider specific behaviors that support generous inclusion and developmental focus. Table 4 provides dos and don'ts to help leaders be effective with these keys to humility.

TABLE 4. "How I Treat You": Recommended Behaviors.

GENEROUS INCLUSION	
DO	**DON'T**
Encourage people to share ideas and feelings on important issues.	Limit participation to minor discussions and routine matters.
Notice when your power may cause others to defer to you unnecessarily, and encourage them to contribute.	Assume that others have little to offer.
Examine your attitudes toward diversity of all kinds.	Allow biases to result in excluding certain types of people.
Listen deeply—even when others present views that seem unfamiliar or uncomfortable.	Ignore others' views or cut people off when they share opinions.
Present an emotionally welcoming demeanor.	Signal that you are too busy or disinterested to interact with others.
DEVELOPMENTAL FOCUS	
DO	**DON'T**
Listen to others' career aspirations.	Ignore others' future ambitions.
Teach, coach, and mentor those around you.	View people as merely present to support your work agenda.
Recognize that leadership and culture affect talent and performance management.	Neglect the cultural health of the "container" you create for working together.
Pay attention to people skills, especially humility, when developing leaders.	Assume drive and knowledge of the job or industry will make someone a good leader.

Generous Inclusion

1. There are many types of diversity, and most of us are more comfortable with some types of people than others. Identify the types of people with whom you are most comfortable and uncomfortable. Think carefully about whether and how your words and actions may exclude those who are different from your preferred group.

2. Think about how you can better *engage* stakeholders you may neglect. Jot down two or three topics in which you believe they have interest, and make notes on where you see opportunities for collaboration. Discuss one of these topics with them, along with parameters for the outcome. Then invite stakeholders to follow up with suggestions on how progress can be made.

3. Conflict can be challenging, but avoiding it can be worse. How do you handle stakeholders who have very different views? Think about how you can host conversations that bring differing parties together, facilitate the sharing of views, and ask for suggestions that embrace all needs. The outcome may not be agreement, but it can allow differing parties to understand the range of views you need to handle, bringing you greater support for your ultimate decisions.

Developmental Focus

1. Do you make a practice of seeing talents and skills in others that can be further developed? Observe carefully, then let them know about a specific strength or potential you see and encourage them to grow. Can you back this up with training opportunities? If not, the attention and support alone show developmental focus.

2. Most of us benefit from connections to others at the right time. Do you offer referrals to people in your network to stakeholders when you learn of relevant needs?

3. Have you ever mentored anyone? What skills and knowledge do you have to offer that others might need? Try to identify someone who might be an appropriate mentee. What are some first steps you can take to turn around and help the next one in line?

When leaders feel and display genuine regard for the dignity of others, engagement and performance from working together tend to increase. Chapters 1 through 3 explained why this is so, and chapters 4 through 6 have explained the six behavioral keys involved in leader humility. Because leading means relationship, and because leader humility is so important for working together, the next chapters show how to put this into practice well.

We'll begin with a comprehensive look at how it can apply to large organizations. Chapter 7, a guest chapter written by Alan Mulally, explains the Working Together Management System, based in leader humility, which he evolved while serving as CEO of Boeing Commercial Airplanes. He later used this same system to save Ford Motor Company (without government bailouts) from near bankruptcy during the Great Recession and bring it to profitable success. This is a carefully engineered, comprehensive approach to leading large, complex, global organizations that shows how the keys to humility can be integrated.

Examining this comprehensive system first allows us to see the elements needed in creating a healthy container for work. We can then show how this system can be scaled down to smaller organizations by adapting many of the principles and practices. Chapter 8 identifies the factors you will need to consider in order to craft the right approach for your own setting; then it describes how a total approach to leadership differs from ones that are more common in generating thriving versus toxic organizations. The chapter closes with a sample of additional organizational policies and practices that support others' dignity.

Chapter 9 provides bios on the CEOs interviewed and explores common threads in how they developed humility. It includes a number of suggestions for developing humility yourself. These activities can be adapted for use in leader training and development courses, as can material in the "Discussion Guide," at the end of the book.

Let's turn now to our guest author, Alan Mulally. We can learn a great deal from his deep experience creating thriving organizations and great results.

CHAPTER SEVEN

Working Together Management System

by Alan Mulally

Work is love made visible.
—Kahlil Gibran

Leadership is truly an honor and responsibility. I have had the opportunity and honor to serve two important American and global icons that deliver valuable products and services for the greater good. Throughout the years, I have been able to contribute to the design, production, and support of the very best airplanes and automobiles in the world. I was later privileged to serve as CEO of Boeing Commercial Airplanes and CEO of the Ford Motor Company through good times as well as crises (the negative impact on the airline industry and Boeing of the 9/11 attacks and similar impact on Ford of the Great Recession).

Over my career, I have found that *the leader's most important contribution is:*

- to hold him- or herself and the leadership team collectively responsible and accountable for

- defining a compelling vision, comprehensive strategy, and relentless implementation

- to deliver value for all the stakeholders.

Development of the organization's mission, vision, and strategy are essential first steps, but they are not enough for leadership. And tracking progress (and knowing what went wrong after the fact) is important and can help avoid mistakes in the future—but that is not enough for leadership either. Boards, employees, investors—and even the voting public—are seeking leaders who do more than explain what went wrong after the fact. They want leaders who can ensure that plans are met successfully. This is why great leaders must be accountable for compelling vision, comprehensive strategy—*and* relentless implementation.

My goal in this chapter is to provide a proven and replicable approach for success that I developed while working with many great teams—our Working Together Management System™ (WTMS, which I will refer to in this chapter simply as Working Together or WT). WT is a powerful process for leading and managing an organization, because it is based on humility, love, and service. It will create a smart, healthy, and continuously improving culture in any organization. It works in both product and service organizations to deliver the products and services that people value with ever-improving productivity.

Because I want to share this unique system with you, let me bring you into my world as I write. Imagine that you and I are actually working together as partners in achieving something significant! To show how we collaborate, I am going to use the term *our* to explain the four major elements of our Working Together Management System:

- Our Creating Value Road Map

- Our Expected Behaviors

- Our Business Plan Review

- Our Leader's Unique Service

Each element of WT is integrated with the others. I will begin by discussing them one at a time, but it is important to understand that they *must* go together to achieve results. Then I'll say more about how the elements interact; how this approach is based on humility, love, and service; and why it is so effective. Let me now describe each of these, beginning with a model of how we create value for all stakeholders, as shown in figure 9.

A great place to start in understanding our WT is that we are *delivering value for all our stakeholders*. We care not only about financial performance and benefits for shareholders, but also about the relationships we have with our customers, employees, suppliers, community, and so on. Notice that our WT has performance measures for each of these! The hopes and dreams of our stakeholders are included in our Vision (shown in the center of this model) as we consider the Broader Context of our business environment, develop our Strategic Plan to achieve the vision, and conduct our Business Plan Review to ensure relentless implementation of our Plan. In other

Business Plan Review
- The Plan
- Status and Forecast
- Risks and Opportunities
- Special Attention
- Better Plan

Broader Context
- World Politics
- Economy
- Energy
- Environment
- Technology
- Labor
- Competition

Performance Measures
- Satisfaction of Customers, Employees, Suppliers, Investors, Community
- Revenue/Margin
- Cash Flow

Strategic Plan
- Performance
- Product
- Process
- People

Business Environment *Vision* *Plan* *Strategy*

FIGURE 9. Our WT Creating Value Road Map.

words, our Vision itself is compelling because it is designed to serve a greater good that delivers real value to all our stakeholders. We are *committed* to creating profitable growth for all. To help achieve this vision, we rely on the three additional elements of WT.

Our WT Principles, Practices, and Expected Behaviors

Critical to the success of WT is a set of principles, practices, and behaviors that, from here on, I will refer to simply as "Expected Behaviors." Because these are the foundation of a smart and healthy organizational culture, I will list them here in table 5, then describe how we will practice them:

TABLE 5. Expected Behaviors.

• People first . . . Love them up.	• Everyone knows the plan, the status, and areas that need special attention.
• Everyone is included.	
• Compelling vision, comprehensive strategy, and relentless implementation.	• Propose a plan, and have a positive, find-a-way attitude.
• Clear performance goals.	• Respect, listen, help, and appreciate each other.
• One Plan.	• Emotional resilience—trust the process.
• Facts and data.	• Have fun—enjoy the journey and each other.

Putting People First

Note that the very first point is "People first." When thinking about implementation, most leaders consider metrics and tracking first. But our success as an organization will ultimately be determined by our ability to work together as a team, including all of the stakeholders, to make the strategy succeed. So, we believe in the dignity of every member of our leadership and employee team. We also believe in the dignity of every stakeholder in our extended enterprise: unions, suppliers, distributors, customers, investors, government, and so on. Saying we believe in other people's dignity is not just lip service. It governs how we behave with each other. Our leadership team is committed to respect, inclusion, transparency, helping, and appreciating every participant.

Engaging people fully, enlisting their creativity and motivation, and inspiring them to work together is critically important. They give their best to their jobs when they really care about us. And they care about us most when we demonstrate that we care about them and that we need and want their hearts and minds. We demonstrate this by showing that we are committed to creating a smart and healthy organizational culture based on our WT principles, practices, and management system. Unfortunately, this is rarely given the recognition it deserves and is a major reason why implementation often fails.

The issue of putting people first will reveal that **who you are is critically important in leadership**. That's because Who I Am has a lot to do with what I do and how I do it. If the leader does not fully believe that all people are valuable enough to contribute significantly to the organization's success, then the leader's views and expectations will adversely affect the culture and results over time. When we truly put people first, this means everyone is included. We need to break down assumptions that only people at the top should know and oversee the organization's strategic efforts. In fact, what we need is transparency—genuine openness—about both what we are trying to accomplish and how we are doing.

And we need to ensure that the views of *everyone* in our extended enterprise—including stakeholders who will be affected by our decisions—has their views represented in our discussions. This applies not only to our supply chain, but to *all* stakeholders, including government legislators and international partners. Rather than have us determine what is best for them and try to force it on them, we work together with them by including them in the development of the strategy and plan. That means we discuss our mutual goals and needs. As an example, every country has its own certification requirements for cars and planes. Differences like this are challenging when we are doing business globally. But by having the humility to include our international partners as we develop our plan (respecting their dignity as well as their views and systems), we are able to work together on compromises acceptable to all sides.

Vision, Strategy, Goals, and Implementation

As leaders, we are collectively responsible and accountable for developing a compelling vision for our organization. What makes it compelling are two things. First, it has to be about the value we are delivering for the greater good. We are providing products and services that improve the lives of others. It is not going to be compelling if it is mainly about profits or about work that is harmful to others. Second, the vision needs to be meaningful for all participants so that they want to commit their talent, energy, and enthusiasm to accomplishing it.

WT also develops a comprehensive strategy to achieve our compelling vision. The strategy will encompass all the elements needed to achieve the vision. Our business performance measures will include profitable growth for the benefit of all the stakeholders. Our goals and the organization's business performance measures will also include ever-increasing customer, employee, supplier, community, union, and investor satisfaction. We examine all performance measures on a rolling five-year window. This allows us to compare how we are doing against past performance, and to balance near- and longer-term investment and performance.

Because leaders are accountable for developing a compelling vision and comprehensive strategy, the vision and strategy need to become the "One Plan" that *everyone* in the organization knows and works to achieve. So, everyone is next involved in defining clear performance goals. Leaders from each business unit and functional skill team of the organization identify what *they* need to do to help achieve the overall vision and strategy. To illustrate this, the head of HR will likely have strategies and plans for people, talent, diversity, training, performance management, compensation, appreciation, etc. The head of sales will have plans for customers, sales, market share, margins, etc. The head of manufacturing will have plans for quality, production, productivity, suppliers, partners, automation, and so on.

Our One Plan also cascades down the organization. So, each member of the leadership team works with his or her managers to create their plans, all of which support our One Plan.

We use facts and data to evaluate progress against our plan, so we ask our team to monitor and share accurate information. We can't manage a secret—and the data sets us free to work together to address the challenges and areas of our plan that need special attention. The data also helps us identify with confidence the opportunities for improvement so that we can focus collaborative efforts and work together on those areas to improve. In this system, everyone knows what the plan is, everyone knows the status at any point in time, and everyone knows the areas that need special attention. Having such a clear picture of our performance allows us to develop an even better plan each year to continuously improve our business performance measures.

The process element (our Business Plan Review, discussed shortly) includes a method for regularly reviewing progress relying on facts and data. However, certain behaviors are essential to moving forward effectively. First, we all must truly respect, listen, help, and appreciate each other. We need and want everyone's very best self: hearts, minds, and working together. We respect the dignity of every participant, and we seek to understand before we seek to be understood.

Meetings must not allow destructive criticism or any jokes at others' expense. And it is critical for the leader to *model* this behavior first by demonstrating full respect, listening, help, and appreciation of all others. The leader must also manage the behavior of people below him or her. That means the leader cannot tolerate words and actions by others that violate the agreed-to Expected Behaviors. If the leader does not address inappropriate behaviors, people will quickly sense that we say "People first" but don't mean it. Once that happens, they are less likely to be motivated to give their all to the organization's goals. And without a safe environment, everyone will hesitate to share the real situation or their thoughts. We will then not know what we need to know. And implementation will suffer because we cannot manage a secret.

As we review progress, we are sure to identify problem areas. Using the WTMS's Expected Behaviors, we propose a plan and have a positive, find-a-way attitude in the face of problems. We believe there is always a way to deliver our plan or develop a better plan going forward. Attitude is everything, and it is infectious, so we stress keeping a positive attitude. Working together, using all of our collective knowledge, always works to deliver the plan or develop the needed, better plan.

Let no improvement in flying pass us by. —BILL BOEING, FOUNDER, THE BOEING COMPANY

If you think you can or think you can't, you are proba-
bly right. —HENRY FORD, FOUNDER, FORD MOTOR COMPANY

Our WT Business Plan Review

The third element of our WT is our Business Plan Review
(BPR). This is a weekly review session—yes, every week.
Our objective for our BPR is that we work as a team to
review *every* element of our plan, our status against the
plan in each person's area of responsibility, and the areas
that need our special attention to get back on plan. Our
BPR objective is *not* to work the solutions or create better
plans for the areas of our plan that need special attention. We work those together as well—but in separate,
regularly scheduled "special attention meetings" that follow our BPR meetings.

Our BPR process clearly describes how we implement
our strategy and plan to accomplish our vision. It also
explains our meetings, our decision process, how we
adapt to our rapidly changing world, and how we manage our risks and opportunities. It is conducted among
the CEO and the head of each business unit (that is,
product or service) and functional skills unit (such as HR,
sales, engineering). Attendance of the entire leadership
team is mandatory because this is critical for our working
together. The BPR informs our decision process and communications with all participants in the extended organization. Guests may be invited but do not participate
in the discussion. We want everyone to know the plan,
the status against the plan, and the areas of the plan
that need our special attention. We also want everyone
to experience the way the entire leadership team works
together on our One Plan.

The meeting begins with the CEO reviewing the Creating Value Road Map or One Plan. The CEO summary presents the plan for the quarter and for the current year, the five-year outlook, and the status/forecast against the plan. In one or two slides, this summary is provided for a number of performance measures, such as profitable growth for all of the organization's stakeholders, and satisfaction of each stakeholder: customers, employees, investors, suppliers, and the communities in which it operates.

Most units will have several subgoals they need to achieve that support the One Plan. Following the CEO's summary, leaders of each unit review the goals agreed to for their part of the organization and what the status is with respect to those goals. For the BPR, leaders code the progress for the week on each of their goals with green, yellow, or red. Green means "on plan." Yellow means "off plan but we have a plan to get back on plan." And red means "off plan and working to develop a plan to get back on plan." As shown in figure 10, one summary chart for the organization quickly conveys to all what the status is compared to our One Plan.

Problems are quickly seen because they are highlighted. As these arise, they are immediately assigned for special attention to take place at a separate meeting prior to the next BPR. Members of the group as a whole also may have suggestions to help resolve them. Plans will be established at the interim meeting for how to improve performance on that indicator. Subsequent reporting will continue to color-code progress on that indicator as people work together to resolve the problems. In that way, problems are quickly identified and worked, and the status will show progress moving from red to yellow, then from yellow to green, in short order.

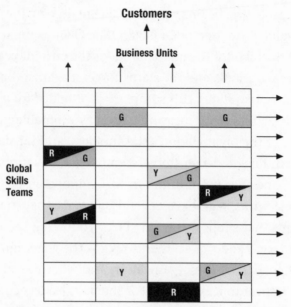

KEY: Last week is shown in the upper left triangle. The current week is shown in the lower right triangle. G = Green; R = Red; Y = Yellow. This chart allows all to quickly understand the status of the whole organization compared to its One Plan.

FIGURE 10. Business Plan Performance Summary of Status versus the Plan.

We treat the new yellow and red items as gems because we expect all of us to identify our gems early so that we all can work together to get them back on plan. We have emotional resilience—we know there will always be gems, so we expect them and expect to deal with them. We show appreciation for the transparency of those who share their gems by offering both a positive reception in the BPR and our collaboration at Special Attention Meetings that follow, where we work together on a recovery plan. We also communicate throughout the organization the status and recovery plans and thank everyone for their contributions.

We trust the process. We trust all elements of WT because we know it works. The BPR is a reliable process for relentless implementation. It allows the leader—and everyone else in the organization—to know where things stand at any point in time. Because the Expected Behaviors are coupled with a reliable process that is using metrics and data, people become confident that we are all working together on One Plan. As problems arise, we all work to resolve them, and we are far more effective and successful together than trying to operate independently.

Our WT Leader's Unique Service

Let me reiterate that a leader's *most important contribution* is to hold him- or herself and the leadership team collectively responsible and accountable for defining a compelling vision, comprehensive strategy, and relentless implementation plan to deliver value for all stakeholders. So, our WT leader's *unique service* is to ensure that all elements of our WTMS are used consistently by everyone: our Creating Value Roadmap, our Expected Behaviors, and our Business Plan Review. The leader and leadership team must not tolerate violations of these elements of WT.

When I say we cannot tolerate violations, I mean no exceptions. If people on the team are not practicing the Expected Behaviors, the leader must have private discussions with them in a timely way to advise them to adapt. If someone isn't sure that he or she wants to or is able to change, I always advise that person, "That's OK. It doesn't mean you're a bad person. But your decision means you are choosing not to be part of our team here."

And if the behavior continues to be a problem—when people prove they are unwilling or unable to adapt after a few discussions—I help them realize that they are making the choice to leave rather than change—and that's OK. The process must have integrity to work; if the leader fails to hold everyone accountable for the process, then we are not working together, and the principles, practices, and behaviors will be seen as a sham. So, our WT leaders' unique service is to ensure the integrity of WT!

Let me add that the leader's character needs to be based on humility, love, and service. And the leader's competencies must shift from command and control to be a role model, a facilitator, and a coach. If you are not comfortable with humility, love, and service as the basis of your leadership, you will have a hard time being a good facilitator and coach, and you will not be able to get the results that this approach delivers.

Working Together is a comprehensive system—a method that has been demonstrated to work and work very well. It can be adapted to many different industries and organizations. As the organization succeeds in its goals, all of the stakeholders succeed.

Applications

I have used our WT in many leadership roles, and it always works. It is so important for the leader to be consistent in being honest and sincere about "People first," "Everyone is included," and "Listen, respect, and help one another." This takes genuine humility as we display deep regard for everyone's dignity. At times, I have found that people don't trust this approach at the start. It takes patience and consistent behavior to build trust and help people understand that we are going to do everything the way WT prescribes it.

One example of this was reported in *American Icon* (2012), in which Bryce Hoffman wrote about the turn-around at Ford Motor Company. In the first few weeks, during our BPRs, everybody's progress reports were all coded green—meaning everything was going according to plan. Of course, I knew that couldn't be accurate. I told them, "You know, we are losing billions of dollars. Isn't there *anything* that's not going well?"

This is a good example of how, as a leader, you just can't manage a secret. Because you have power, people generally tell you what they think you want to hear. If they don't feel safe revealing problems, they usually won't. A lot of times, leaders will say they are open but will criticize someone when problems show up, and that quickly cuts down on the upward flow of information.

It took a little while longer at Ford, but Mark Fields was the first person to show vulnerability. He had decided to hold off the launch of the Ford Edge, a highly anticipated product, because testing had found a grinding noise in the suspension but could not identify its cause. And he decided to share that in the BPR. Hoffman (2012, 124) described Mark's report in the BPR:

> "And, on the Edge launch, we're red. You can see it there," he said, pointing at the screen. "We're holding the launch." Everyone turned toward Fields. So did Mulally, who was sitting next to him.
>
> *Dead man walking*, thought one of his peers.
>
> Suddenly, someone started clapping. It was Mulally.

"Mark, that is great visibility," he beamed. "Who can help Mark with this?"

Bennie Fowler raised his hand. He said he would send some of his quality experts to Oakville right away. Tony Brown, Ford's vice president in charge of purchasing, said he would contact all the relevant suppliers and ask them to check their components.

Like so many others, this problem was resolved by having someone *trust the process* enough to bring it forward—and by having us work together to resolve it quickly. But people were also watching Mark—and me, as the leader. They thought he was taking a real risk by sharing that problem, so the next week he was still the only one willing to do that. When he had not been criticized or dismissed after the second meeting, people saw that I really wanted transparency and that we were really going to live up to our Expected Behaviors. So, at the next BPR, the leadership team brought a set of slides mixed with yellow and red, as well as green. We could finally get down to the business of helping Ford.

Let me note how well this example shows how extraordinarily powerful the leader humility model (in chapter 3) really is. I'll briefly illustrate three connections here:

1. "Who I Am" as a leader was essential for us to make this kind of progress. The members of the leadership team had to see that I had a balanced ego and integrity in order to trust the process enough to disclose the problems we were facing. If they had found me arrogant or believed my comments about working together were

only lip service, they would have remained self-protective. A sea of green reports would have led us straight into bankruptcy because you can't manage a secret.

2. "The Direction I Set" was also essential to our success. Our vision was compelling and our strategy was ethical because they served a larger good: profitable growth for all stakeholders. Our One Plan engaged everyone enthusiastically.

3. "How I Treat You" was equally powerful because it relied on our Expected Behaviors. Everyone was included—everyone understood the plan and participated in it. Our inclusion was generous and genuine. The use of One Plan, along with the BPR process that cascades down, was also developmentally focused. It taught all the organization's leaders more about the business —and about how to run the business. People could see their role in our work, the value they brought to the team, and how they would personally thrive as a result of working together.

In my consulting, I have heard a number of complaints about leadership and cultures. This one shows how problems usually begin:

[T]hings start to deteriorate when the leader's behavior becomes erratic during difficult situations. Tempers flare, bullying starts, and the mode becomes looking for someone to blame when issues surface.

Sadly, this creates an environment of fear and intimidation. It shows that the leader lacks the humility to genuinely respect the dignity of others. Over the years, I have received many, many comments from people about how unusual our WT process is, how well it works, and why it works. Let me share just a few of them here:

- "It starts with a leader that creates the environment for working together and leads by example."

- "PEOPLE are central to working together. And that means everyone. You and key leaders lived that every day—people knew they mattered."

- "The primary difference [in] the One Plan environment we created revolves around creating a culture of trust, transparency and accountability that didn't exist before. The genesis of that successful environment started with your willingness to reach out to all constituencies and be a good listener. Under your guidance, we listened better, gathered facts and efficiently used data to craft the One Plan."

- "If the leader doesn't live and breath[e] it and a few members of the leadership team are jockeying for position to take over, the negative effect on the culture will follow. I remember you saying if someone could not get on board with the changes you were making, it was OK, they could leave, and you had to ask a few to do so."

- "Having a comprehensive plan that everyone could work on and believe in created a force multiplier rooted in trust. What I learned is that, even during the worst of times, a good plan with inspirational leadership will motivate your partners to run through a wall for the good of the team."

- "Everyone knew the plan and through the cascaded BPR system understood their role in it. But what's more they understood the WHY. Critical especially for the tough decisions."

- "Special attention reviews at the right place at the right time with the right people."

- "You inspired us to do more and be more than we ever thought possible."

Our WT really works. It is based on humility, love, and service. The leader has to have humility to deeply respect the dignity of others. When I say, "People first—love them up," I mean that. We use the word *love* too narrowly and need to genuinely care about the people we lead. They are not just pawns to be used to achieve goals, but human beings—love them up! Show them they matter. And when you focus on serving the greater good, and invite them to join you in doing that, they will bring their hearts and minds and give it all they have.

All the elements of our WT interact to support high performance and smart and healthy organizations. For instance, "Everyone is included" and having One Plan makes it possible for all of us to be working in the same direction. Requiring the Expected Behaviors of "Listen, respect, and help one another" supports "Everyone knows the plan, the status of the plan, and the areas that need special attention" because, as the example with Mark Fields showed, people will only be transparent when the environment is safe. So, each of the Expected Behaviors is critical because they interact powerfully.

Working Together is so effective because people come alive when their dignity is respected. They know they matter, and we are all engaged together in doing something really meaningful for the greater good. Working together on a strategy and plan to deliver a compelling vision for the benefit of all the stakeholders and the greater good is really satisfying and fun! Feeling the satisfaction of the individual's and team's meaningful accomplishment and service is to live. Humility, love, and service work for the greater good. WT allows for adapting, growing, and thriving in our rapidly changing world. Working Together always works!

CHAPTER EIGHT

The Art and Practice of Humility

The miracle is this—the more we share, the more we have.
—Leonard Nimoy

In writing about leader humility, my point is not to suggest that leaders should somehow be more dazzling or lenient. Humility does not require charisma or low standards. My intent is to showcase the extraordinary power of humility for *working together*, thereby creating thriving organizations and great results. There can be no doubt that Alan Mulally's Working Together Management System (WTMS) did this at Boeing and Ford. Central to his approach is the unique role of the leader, and it is one based in humility.

You might be wondering whether it can work for you if your organization is smaller or if your leadership responsibilities are different or less complex. I believe it can, and I explain below how this approach can scale to different situations. Following that, I'll share more about how humility looks in practice at the organizational level, beginning with a big-picture view of how Total Leaders (those with strong drive and humility) generate healthy, high-performing organizations—and concluding with examples of other organizational policies that support humility and performance.

Scaling for Smaller Size

The WTMS has a number of elements that generalize to organizations of any size. These include: (1) embracing the leader's most important responsibility, (2) identifying the Creating Value Road Map, and (3) establishing behavioral norms for working together. A fourth element, the structure and process for how you oversee the work (ensuring implementation), can easily be adapted to varied circumstances. Let me discuss each of these in turn.

#1—Leader's Responsibility

Mulally states that the leader's most important contribution is to hold him- or herself and the team collectively responsible and accountable for defining a compelling vision, comprehensive strategy, and relentless implementation. You'll recall that defining compelling vision and ethical strategies are two of the keys to leader humility. I have said that the leader creates the container, and Mulally clearly places responsibility on the leader to create the direction, processes, and culture that determine how we work together to deliver value for all stakeholders. He sees this as the "leader's unique service."

This *most important contribution* applies to leaders of any organizational size, not only to large organizations like Ford and Boeing. The leader's unique role applies to entrepreneurial start-ups, midsized family businesses, the local neighborhood store, and community organizations. It also applies to leaders of skill functions like finance or human resources, and to those overseeing product divisions. And it applies to nonprofit and government organizations offering an extremely wide range of services, such as health care, education, or veterans' services, to name just a few. It even applies to leaders who govern.

So, the number one issue in the success of WTMS and in scaling it to smaller or different types of organizations is understanding and accepting that the leader's most important responsibility is creating and maintaining the container for work. When leaders understand how significant this is, they can be mindful and smart about the rest.

#2—Identifying Your Creating Value Road Map

Every organization exists to add value. Leaders need to guide the organization in identifying the best path to create value for *all* the organization's stakeholders. Figure 9 showed a road map for creating value at Ford Motor Company. What if you are running an urgent-care clinic? Or a small copy and mailing center? Or a computer repair shop? You still create value and need to know what that is, who is affected, and what the best strategies are to create and manage results for all your stakeholders.

As one example, a couple starting a computer-repair shop might have an initial goal of providing repair services for customers. Quickly, they discover that they will need more technical staff and facilities to provide some requested services, along with administrative staff to conduct intake questions and process billing. They will need to decide exactly which services to provide and what their average turnaround time and pricing will be. Yet, if they step back and examine the broader context, they will likely notice competitors in the local market—not only for the same services, but for the talent they need to hire. They'll see that there is also some risk of damage or data loss that requires insurance and legal advice. Cost-benefit analyses can help these leaders identify a path to profitability.

Looking even more closely, we see that the store's reputation and success depend on the satisfaction of customers who give referrals and bring repeat business. Yet customers and the local community both are impacted by a challenging parking situation around the store. And perhaps some repairs require replacement components that are hard to secure and for which the store needs a reliable vendor. The leaders should recognize that stakeholders include not only employees but customers, community members, and vendors. Integrating all their needs should be considered in the Creating Value Road Map. This might lead to vision and strategy statements that reflect their path to creating value, such as "We provide quality repairs for customers at affordable prices and quick turnaround, and we validate their parking in a nearby garage. We offer strong wages and working conditions for our employees, and incentives to our vendors for being reliable." The leaders and team can then create an appropriate work stream for implementing their vision and strategy and agree on performance goals and measures for achieving the desired results.

Importantly, measures need to address the interests of all stakeholders. This requires the keys of generous inclusion and developmental focus of humility. By assessing our impact on all stakeholders, we move beyond lip service. That is, we *draw the boundary so that all who are affected by our work are on the inside; their needs and concerns must be actively incorporated in our vision, strategy, and measurement.* In this example, the leaders should monitor costs and revenue, average turnaround time for repair, customer delight (with work quality, timeliness, and parking), vendor satisfaction, and community concerns about parking impact. Having a clear sense of how value is created and how to measure progress toward implementation is important—and doable—for organizations of any size.

#3—Establishing Behavioral Norms for Working Together

WTMS is explicit about Expected Behaviors. Many of these are specific interpersonal behaviors that are closely tied to the subject of this book: leader humility. And they illustrate how a leader's use of the keys to humility—and the leader's insistence that everyone else behave that way—generate a healthy culture for working together. This includes the keys to leader humility of balanced ego and integrity. "People first—love them up," "Everyone is included," "Respect, listen, help, and appreciate each other," "Emotional resilience—trust the process," "Propose a plan, and have a positive, find-a-way attitude," and "Have fun—enjoy the journey and each other" are all behaviors that are based in leader humility because they show deep regard for the dignity of others. When these behaviors are modeled by the leader, and when others are expected to demonstrate these same behaviors, the organization becomes open, trusting, thriving. Importantly, these behaviors scale completely—they can be applied to any size organization.

#4—Structure and Process for Ensuring Implementation

Another set of the Expected Behaviors (figure 9) is what I consider practices for managing the work or overseeing implementation. Some of these I discussed in #1 and #2 above: how the leader's acceptance of his or her most important responsibility as a leader, and then identifying the road map for creating value, can both be scaled to smaller organizations. That should result in a compelling vision, a comprehensive strategy, performance goals, and measures. WTMS also emphasizes having One Plan that everyone is working together on, where "Everyone knows the plan, the status, and the areas that need attention." These scale very well to organizations of any size. The use of facts and data to assess progress should apply to organizations of any size because data refers to the key indicators that need to be monitored regularly to ensure successful implementation. Data can be quantitative or qualitative, and it can be gathered formally or informally, as appropriate.

Finally, we come to the structure for how leaders monitor implementation. Mulally's Business Plan Review (BPR) is a weekly status meeting (with interim meetings to address concerns that arise), and the process of using color-coded slides to summarize progress ensures that everyone involved knows the plan, the status, and the areas that need special attention. The format and structure involved in the BPR for WTMS is a well-engineered practice. It is extremely effective at allowing the leader and team to maintain steady oversight of a very large, global, multiproduct organization with many stakeholders.

What if your organization has just five people? What if, instead of being spread out globally, you work together daily in an 800-square-foot office? Or perhaps you have fifty employees across two sites in the same city? Or five hundred people providing three different services? Perhaps you consider yourself midmarket in size with fifteen hundred employees. What structure is appropriate then?

In all cases, points #1, #2, and #3 above should apply well to your organization. You should still ensure that everyone knows the plan and its status. Also, you will need a way of monitoring progress that the team and you, as the leader, understand and follow to ensure implementation. But the structure for how you and they stay current can to be adapted to fit your work. There are many ways that can look, but here are some important questions to ask:

- How many people need to coordinate with you and each other? In general, larger staff means more communication nodes. It adds complexity that gets harder to oversee informally. Four to eight people can often interact very well informally; many organizations are of this size. Yet, as we approach ten to fifteen people, lapses in communication tend to occur, and this can hurt results.

- What is the physical proximity of this group? Are they all in one place or dispersed? Small teams who interact with each other daily because they are together can usually keep communications going well.

- How frequently do they naturally come in contact? Even if the team is small—if it's composed of outside salespeople, for example—having offices in the same space doesn't ensure needed information exchange.

- Where is the leader in physical relation to the entire team? And how often is the leader present with the team? Having a headquarters office while managing a remote branch puts the leader at risk of missing important information. And being away on frequent travel or out with clients 90 percent of the time differs from being present with the team half time every day.

- If the organization is small, what degree of overlap exists in team members' jobs, and who among them needs what information to do their jobs well? A small organization may have five or ten people working on a common goal but with distinct responsibilities and very little overlap in what they do. Frequent meetings for status sharing will have less relevance in that type of situation than for a group of five or more who need to exchange and receive information to conduct their individual work effectively.

- What is the pace of change on the measures you are tracking? If you are concerned about sales in a brick-and-mortar retail store, you would not want to go a month before learning that sales were down year over year. Weekly or biweekly meetings are appropriate. If you lead a small, boutique consulting group, and securing government contracts takes a protracted period of time, significant change is not likely each week.

- What about the temperaments, motivation, personalities, and skill levels among your team? For skilled, highly motivated teams who exhibit the right behaviors when working together, depending on the leader's needs as well, less oversight may be appropriate. For teams that struggle with each other, or where members are not well trained or very motivated, frequent interaction with the leader is important.

Creating a structure for overseeing implementation will be up to you, but recall that the leader's most important responsibility includes holding self and team accountable not only for vision and strategy but for implementation. So, getting team input is recommended because it supports their dignity, and you should agree on the practice you will use to track implementation regularly.

At one end, there is the highly structured BPR that meets weekly. I recommend this for organizations that are moderate to large in size and complexity. For very small organizations, the questions above should help leaders determine what's needed. A team of four or five people who interact continually in the same physical office, with the leader present as well, can typically communicate what it needs to know in real time. A separate structure (such as BPR) is generally not needed. Assuming that team members are skilled and fully engaged in the One Plan approach, and the norms of humility prevail, the organization can thrive on informality. This works well for many leaders of dynamic, small groups.

Other leaders prefer more structure. And organizations whose size and complexity are not so small (more than ten to twelve on the team) typically need a structured approach. Leaders and the group benefit from a regular meeting of staff to focus on specific implementation measures. WTMS provides a strong model for this. The questions above should help you decide what type of structure you need in order to manage implementation well.

Big Picture—Best Practices

Whether your organization is large, midsized, or small, the humility-based principles presented thus far create healthy containers for work. Let me now provide the big-picture overview of how leader humility creates thriving organizations and how the lack of leader humility can be toxic enough to produce harmful results.

Research has signaled for some time just how important leader humility is. Collins (2001) reported an in-depth comparison of organizations that became great (based on profits, stock performance, etc.) versus those that were merely good. The most important difference proved to be *leadership*. Intriguingly, while we might expect charisma to be important, it was *humility* that was found to be one of two differentiators of organizational performance. "Great" organizations had leaders who possessed both: fierce resolve for success and personal humility. Collins (2005) described this as "Level 5" leadership.

I am going to refer to leaders who combine strong drive with humility as the "Total Leader" because I'll be distinguishing their impact from something that arises when humility is missing: toxicity. Drawing on his explanation of WTMS in chapter 7, let me use Alan Mulally as an example of a Total Leader to explain figure 11. His drive was focused on the whole organization: he used One Plan and weekly Business Plan Reviews to set direction and drive implementation. In addition, his genuine humility was evident. The Expected Behaviors he required of himself and his full leadership team (no exceptions) displayed deep regard for others' dignity. As others' dignity was supported, collaboration and performance increased, and organizations thrived under his leadership. As we should expect based on Collins (2001), the combination of strong drive and leader humility produced great results.

Because this has been true for all the CEOs I interviewed, you can see that humility is incredibly powerful. Much like a secret sauce, when coupled with drive, a leader's humility builds a self-reinforcing system, as shown in figure 11. It enhances others' dignity and collaboration and performance. Heightened enthusiasm and performance create a thriving dynamic in the organization, which provides positive feedback to the leader (appreciation and reputation), which in turn reinforces both the leader's drive and humility.

But what happens when leaders are lacking in one of the elements that Collins (2001) found to be important? Well, if a leader has humility but lacks drive, the organization will tend not to advance well (which is bad for long-term performance). However, we tend to select leaders who are driven. We want them to be driven because we assume that their drive for results will lead to great performance. As a result, few senior leaders seem to lack

FIGURE 11. The Thriving Organization.

drive. Instead, a much more common scenario is one in which leaders are driven—but lack humility. What happens then?

When leaders have strong drive that is not tempered by humility, very different organizational cultures—and different results—occur. Although there is certainly a range of these behaviors, from slight to moderate to extreme, figure 12 shows the *direction of the effect* of · leader drive without humility on organizations. Many people describe leaders who are strongly lacking in humility, and the organizational cultures that result, as being "toxic." Toxic leaders direct their drive at others—exhorting them to perform, primarily through power and control (sometimes through fear and intimidation).

The lack of leader humility triggers a downward spiral because it damages others' dignity. Not being seen as individuals whose dignity matters, others feel used and disregarded. Lower morale and motivation result, causing leaders to drive others harder, sometimes berating them for not meeting goals. Mistrust rises, internal cross talk and complaining increases, and political behavior grows as people try to protect and defend themselves. Bystanders hear of complaints about leaders and learn to be on guard for mistreatment. These create such a toxic brew that organizational satisfaction and engagement decline, performance declines, and cynicism about leadership increases. The organization as a whole becomes toxic instead of high performing.

These models clarify why leader humility is so important for generating thriving organizations. Leader humility *personally and directly* affects the dignity of others, having an effect on engagement, performance, and satisfaction. When we recall from chapter 1 that Gallup (2018) found that 66 percent of employees are only minimally engaged cognitively and emotionally in their work, that they show up but do the minimum required, we need to examine the role of leaders in creating the container

FIGURE 12. The Toxic Organization.

for working together. When the container is unhealthy, people may stay but they disengage. The same tendency occurs with other stakeholders: when the leader is toxic, when he or she lacks humility and disregards others' dignity, many stakeholders will withdraw their support (partially or entirely). Working together is harmed and progress slows.

However, the humility of senior leaders can also influence the organization through the *policies and practices* they establish. In addition to WTMS, there are a number of other good practices that support dignity, some dealing with organizational vision and others tied to human resource policies around leader selection, development, compensation, and performance management. Although each organization needs to determine the policies that best fit its needs, I will share several humility-based *best practices* for you to consider.

Organizational Vision

Compelling vision and strategy are not only important keys to leader humility at the unit level but also a great starting point for humility-based policies and practices for the whole organization. As noted in chapter 5, Business Roundtable (2019) has reframed the purpose of business to focus on stakeholder value, not mere shareholder return. And Investopedia (2019) reported that investments are growing rapidly in organizations that are viewed favorably in their approach to environmental, social, and governance impact. Some organizations are broadening their visions accordingly; others need to do so.

Not only are the products, services, and competitive positioning important for investors and customers; organizations will not excel unless employees enjoy being there. What are we doing? What do we stand for? Is this something about which people can feel proud?

Many people have multiple choices about where they can work. If they take pride in the reputation of working for an organization, they will advance your reputation as well as contribute their best. When people look in the mirror, many also will question whether their work environment is adding positively to their reputation. Humility in leadership helps keep you on your toes so that they answer yes. If your organization is weak in this area, you should consider developing additional products, services, or contribution to the greater good that can improve your overall focus. If your products and services, and the way you conduct your business, are all wholesome, you have taken the first important step toward having a positive effect on people working there.

> We are fortunate at Brooks Running because running is a positive force in people's lives. I want people to work at Brooks because they opt into the values of our brand, our business, and how we do our work. —JIM WEBER

Leader Selection

A powerful set of policies and practices that are influenced by an organization's leaders are those for selecting leadership talent. This begins at the board level because boards of directors select both the CEO and other board members. Data show that corporate boards tend to lack diversity in race and gender. In itself, this implies that board members are not practicing generous inclusion (an important aspect of humility) when they do not really see people who differ from the dominant model as being appropriate for invitation.

Homogeneous boards miss out on the value of having diverse views represented in their discussions. Diversity in the employee or customer base should be reflected at higher levels, including the board, to ensure that implications of strategic and competitive directions are thoroughly explored. Diverse membership also brings attention to people issues and inclusion, which are aspects of humility-based leadership. Consider this perspective from a CEO with substantial board experience:

> Diversity definitely helps on boards. If I'm on a board and there's another woman, the discussion is generally more comprehensive. Women tend to look at people and social issues—they'll consider equity, and the diversity lens. The board table also becomes more inclusionary, collaborative. Women help connect the dots for the good of the whole. —PHYLLIS CAMPBELL

Boards of directors typically choose CEOs to lead the organization. So, if the board is inclusive and attentive to humility issues, we might expect it to value this in selecting CEOs. Also, practices in leader selection extend far beyond boards. The CEO and his or her leadership team also need to make humility an important factor in their choice of other leaders in the organization.

> I'm always hiring for culture. It's important that the people we hire can keep their egos in check, be good team leaders, and genuinely like people. It's OK to be proud of your own accomplishments, but you've got to appreciate that others have accomplishments, too. Our culture is strong, such that if people came here selfishly for their own résumé, the organization would quickly sense that, and then chew them up and spit them out. —JIM WEBER

The CEOs I interviewed recognize that humility is not the only important factor in hiring leaders. But they generally placed it prominently in their considerations. Some saw humility as a factor that supported long-term growth in leadership:

> When we hire executives, we tend to hire not just for today. We're betting on that person for the next ten or more years. So, we want someone that is not only good today, but who will just get better over time. And we think humble people do this. Humility helps people develop faster, and they are more fun to be around. There are other qualities we look for also. We're looking for folks who are smart and have the right kind of ambition—for the team and company as opposed to themselves. Finally, they need to be committed, we say "clipped in," to our values. —BRAD TILDEN

Leader Development

Beyond leader selection, other policies and practices should address how organizations will develop future leaders. Three types of learning are especially important. The first is commonly recognized as a need to understand the business. Second, progress into advanced leadership typically benefits from external exposure that builds deeper knowledge in certain skills or broader knowledge of relevant industries and practices.

However, when it comes to leadership development, understanding the business and industry is not enough. An important third area of development is that of a leader's social-emotional skills. This area of competence is too often neglected and can result in toxic organizations. As I have shown in the six keys to humility, the abilities involved in supporting others' dignity are critical, and smart organizations consider this when developing leaders. It can be made explicit as part of succession planning and internal advancement too:

> At Ford, and at Boeing, I always put a factor in our succession planning and performance management about humility. I actually used the word "humility." Is this a person who seeks to understand before being understood? It was a significant factor in decisions for advancement. —ALAN MULALLY

The six keys to leader humility are very important, and most leaders can develop reasonable competence in each if motivated to do so. Nonetheless, nuanced judgment about when to use these keys and how to tailor them will be best when someone's natural *tendency* is to feel and display deep regard for others' dignity. If this tendency is seriously lacking, it may well pose problems over time because leaders face so many complex and challenging situations involving people. Wise CEOs take actions that prevent their cultures from becoming toxic:

> [*Thoughtfully*] It's very difficult to teach "people skills." When we name managers, we have to feel pretty confident that they have good people skills. Certainly, we've made some mistakes. We like to think we're developing a culture that's "jerk free." If someone hates his boss, you get turnover. We've seen some situations where we've turned people around, but if they are not responsive after a couple of tries, you need to move them to a job where they have less supervision of people.
> —JIM SINEGAL

Leadership coaching is one practice that can help develop people skills—if those receiving it are open to growth. The coaching can be informal (through mentoring) or more formal (hiring an outside coach). But part of coaching's success will rest on the organization setting clear expectations that humility is important not only to leadership, but to success in the organization itself. Then leaders who are being coached will understand that humility is not merely a desirable quality but something they must develop as a fundamental leadership competency.

> We've had situations where someone had the technical skills to succeed but needed improvement in humility to handle a senior position. You have to think through that very carefully because you want to balance opportunity for an individual with what's best for everyone else—not just in terms of the skills to do a job but humility and skill in dealing with people. Humility is not the only factor, but it's a very important one. And it's important to be open and frank with a job candidate about the expectation for humility in how they interact with people. I have let people know that, if they fail on that part of the job, it will be career limiting.
> —JEFF MUSSER

Because it can be hard to teach people skills, the executives interviewed were mindful of this when discussing humility. Some take an assertive stance on this when developing leaders: in particular, they look for an individual's *self-awareness*. If that is present, coaching and feedback hold much more promise as part of leader development.

People who don't have insight into their behavior are very difficult to change. People who have humility are generally sensitive to how they interact with others. So, we select for it, and we also train for it, through feedback and coaching. We need people with self-awareness and humility who are open to criticism and guidance. If they lack that openness, they won't be very successful in leadership. —JOHN NOSEWORTHY, MD

Progressive Compensation Approaches

There is wide recognition that income disparities have grown dramatically in the United States since the 1950s, when CEOs made twenty times the salary of the average worker. *Forbes* (Hembree 2018) reported that, for 2017, the multiple had grown so that CEOs made an average of nearly $14 million a year at an S&P Index firm, or 361 times the pay of rank-and-file workers. As the middle class has declined, a number of problems have ensued. Recognizing the dignity of workers, some organizations have used progressive approaches to compensation issues.

One of the more innovative approaches is that of Gravity Payments. In 2015, CEO Dan Price set the minimum salary for its employees in Seattle (an expensive city for housing, etc.) to $70,000 on hearing concerns that some employees were struggling to pay rent along with student loans. He believed that everyone deserved a living wage and slashed his own million-dollar pay package to pay for it. Having recently opened an office in Boise after acquiring the Idaho company ChargeItPro and finding that most employees there were making less than $30,000 per year, Price immediately granted those employees a $10,000 raise and promised to give annual increases that would ensure that everyone was making

$70,000 by 2023 (Hahn 2019). Price was influenced to adopt this minimum income approach by a study that reported that additional money could foster significantly more happiness in the lives of people who made less than $70,000. Price's decision clearly said "I see you" to his employees. Having cut his own pay to provide better wages for them is a form of generous inclusion—he showed deep regard for others' dignity by sharing the wealth. Although he has drawn some criticism for his decision, his company fares well, and his workers report he has made a big difference in their lives.

Other approaches align bonuses and 401(k) contributions to organizational performance. In itself, this is not unusual. What is noteworthy is how the CEOs interviewed were intentional in aligning policies in ways that recognized the contributions of those who did the work and made sure the compensation approach supported their dignity. One of these is Expeditors International, known for strong growth and financial performance, as well as exceptional customer service in its industry. Employees are highly motivated by the way the company's approach to compensation supports their dignity:

> [A] sense of humility shows up in some of our policies. For example, we expect the CEO to pay for parking in the garage just like everyone else. And we give back 25 percent of pre-tax profit to the operating units. About 5 percent goes to cover regional costs, but 20 percent goes to bonus pay in each branch and is allocated to employees—the people who get the work done. Another example is a recent change to our 401(k) plan in which the company used to match $.50 per dollar on the first $3K. We considered going to $.50 per dollar on more—such as

the first $6K. But we decided to go dollar for dollar on the first $3K because it would not disadvantage lower-level employees who can't contribute as much. —JEFF MUSSER

A point worth noting in Musser's example is the company's attention to executive perks with the intent to minimize displays of status favoritism. Several other companies showed this too. Employees reported that Jim Sinegal did not have a reserved parking space. Howard Behar commented that, for many years, Starbucks's policy did not offer company cars for executives. These are all examples of how organizational policies can create distance or suggest collaboration between workers and leaders.

The other point worth noting in Musser's example is how carefully leaders need to think about all employees, whether part-time or full-time, when considering bonus and 401(k) arrangements. Taking this a step further, one of the CEOs interviewed described a thoughtful approach to compensation changes:

> Early in my tenure at REI, we changed our incentive
> plan to include all employees—not just managers.
> Historically, REI had a generous contribution of up to
> 20 percent of salary to employee 401(k) plans for full-
> time employees, and an additional incentive plan for
> managers. But part-time staff, who comprised about
> half of the workforce, had no opportunity to partici-
> pate. There was a disconnect for employees, especially
> part-timers, and we wanted to align their interests with
> those of REI.
>
> So, we changed our practices to reflect a greater
> incentive for all full- and part-time employees to
> achieve our objectives. The 401(k) program was

reshaped to guarantee participating employees 5 percent of their salary, plus an additional 10 percent tied to REI performance overall. We took the remaining 5 percent and funded a performance-based incentive plan for everyone, tied to a combination of their work group's performance and the organization as a whole. That rewarded teamwork, giving all employees line of sight to what they could control, and allowed them to share in the company's success.

This and other changes came by really listening to people—like what makes a living wage—and we began changing our practices to meet their concerns. It was personally humbling and enlightening to see the inconsistencies between our vision and practices. —SALLY JEWELL

In the retail sector, especially in quick-service food and beverage organizations, entry-level wages are low, and turnover is quite high. Starbucks is well known for having broken industry norms decades ago when it offered benefits to part-time workers. This made good strategic sense because it allowed the company to be more selective in hiring, and it reduced turnover. It also generated greater commitment to customer service in a company whose growth depended on that. This arose from people being treated with dignity—being seen as individuals who were important to the company and not as expendable workers.

Currently, a growing concern among employees is for policies that support parenting. Particularly in technology and professional service organizations, employees have wide professional choices and opt for organizations that offer parental leave. Leaders are showing humility in establishing policies that support families:

At TIAA, we strive for human-centered/employee-centered policies. In 2018, we implemented four months of paid leave for new parents. It's for all employees, both full-time and part-time, regardless of their gender, whether or not they physically gave birth, and whether they will be the primary or the secondary caregiver of their child. It was expensive for us to do that, but we did it because we believe it was the right thing to do for our employees and their families. In financial services, your assets leave on the elevator every night. There's a real war for talent out there. You need to show that you value people. —ROGER FERGUSON

Performance Management

A final area of policies and practices concerning leaders is how they are held accountable for performance. There are many ways organizations can do this, but serious attention needs to be given to humility-based behaviors to create a thriving culture. One approach is that of a trial period before a formal commitment is made:

When people are recruited to join the Mayo Clinic, they are given a three-year appointment. Part of that is to see if they fit, and they must be voted on for a permanent appointment. We are all in this for a higher purpose: to improve the health of patients. We look for humility as well as excellence and commitment. —JOHN NOSEWORTHY, MD

A final approach I will mention here involves tightly connecting leaders' compensation to all significant organizational goals (not just some of them, as is commonly done). To illustrate how this can be done well, Alan Mulally used a Performance Management Process (PMP)

as an adjunct to his Working Together Management System. PMP was designed to help leadership team members align their functional contributions and working-together behaviors with the WT system. Each team member would have his or her own plan for individual improvement, as well as responsibility to support other team members and the company's One Plan. The organization's compensation plan for leaders created a strong incentive to meet *all* those needs through the following formula:

Leader's yearly bonus = Leader's target bonus × company performance score × individual performance score

The leader's target bonus is a percentage of the leader's base salary and reflects his or her current responsibilities. The company performance score reflects the company's collective performance on its One Plan. And the individual performance score reflects the person's performance on both functional responsibilities and Expected Behaviors in the WT plan. This last element, the individual performance score, was formed by the leader *and* the team assessing together each leader's individual performance score (that is, there is both peer and individual input).

Each element in the formula is rated from 0 to 2, with 2 being high. The multiplicative nature of the formula means that failure (a 0 rating) on any one element results in no bonus for the year. This system clearly holds leaders accountable for their performance—on Expected Behaviors as well as functional competence. In so doing, it ensures a culture of humility that supports peer collaboration and cascades down to others in the organization.

In sum, leaders' direct behavior affects others' dignity. And leaders' indirect behavior influences others' dignity through the policies and practices that leaders establish. Among the most important are those that affect the selection, development, compensation, and performance management of all leaders in the organization. Collectively, leadership teams implement policies that affect all others, creating thriving (or toxic) organizations.

IDEAS FOR ACTION

1. On a 5-point scale, with 1 meaning very weak and 5 being outstanding, evaluate your own performance on the leader's most important contribution (holding self and team collectively responsible and accountable for generating compelling vision, comprehensive strategy, and relentless implementation).

2. Can you describe for everyone working with you how value is created in what you do? Do they understand who all of your stakeholders are?

3. Using a 5-point scale, rate your organization from 1 (toxic) to 5 (thriving).

4. Do you model the six keys to humility? Do you hold others in your work environment accountable for doing the same?

5. Consider the bullet points in the section "#4—Structure and Process for Ensuring Implementation." What structure and process do you have in place to monitor implementation? Does it need to change? If so, how and why?

CHAPTER NINE

The Formation of Leader Humility

When the heart is touched by direct experience,
the mind may be challenged to change.

—Peter Hans Kolvenbach

The twelve CEOs interviewed for this book provide excellent insights into the value of humility in leadership. They are also remarkable people. Why is it that some leaders have humility and others do not? Since humility is so important, can we understand more about how it is formed? And is there anything we can do to develop it in leaders who lack humility and in others who want to improve their own?

In this chapter, I'll offer several observations on how humility can be formed based on interviews held with the CEOs. Then I'll share my experience in building humility through executive education and consulting, followed by a section containing reflections and activities to improve personal humility. At the end of this chapter, you will also find a page dedicated to each of the CEOs.

These pages contain their exceptional bios and brief statements about how they developed personal humility.

Humility Formation among Interviewees

As I talked with each CEO, I was struck by his or her humility—not only in how each of them interacted with me but also in the genuine regard for stakeholders that came through in their comments. I could not help but wonder how these leaders had developed and maintained personal humility, despite their exceptional responsibilities and accomplishments. Let me briefly describe some themes I observed across my interviews. These include direct experiences, learning from observation, and social norming.

Direct Experience

People whose demographic status falls outside the dominant group become aware of their differences early and tend to experience being unaccepted or not fully fitting in. The experience of being on the outside, being marginalized, will often (though not always) support the development of personal humility. By definition, marginalized groups receive cultural signals that people like them are not as valued. They tend to have to work harder to find their way. When developed appropriately, their mature identity remains aware of their humble roots and has empathy for the dignity of others.

Many aspects of diversity can cause this, but gender and race/ethnicity receive prominent attention precisely because they create significant marginalization. It is still rare for women and minorities to rise to CEO roles in prominent organizations. *Fortune* (Zillman 2019) reported that 6.6 percent of Fortune 500 companies had female CEOs, and *Fortune* (Donnelly 2018) reported that 3 percent of its top 500 firms were headed by African Americans. These numbers guarantee fewer CEO role models like themselves for women and minorities who have the talent and desire to pursue senior positions, and potentially less access to support (such as mentoring and development opportunities).

Several of my interviewees have diverse backgrounds and direct experiences of being in the minority. Phyllis Campbell and Sally Jewell are women—both trailblazers for entering business and management ranks at a time when women had even less access to senior roles. Phyllis is also Asian American (of Japanese descent). As she described in her interview, she had to overcome stereotypes that people have of Asian women. In a similar way, as African American men, Roger Ferguson and Orlando Ashford both needed to find their way in a business world with very few senior executives like them. Members of groups that have faced discrimination generally retain awareness of the ways that demographic distinctiveness places them in the minority. This generally fosters humility.

Let me note that *diversity is but one type of direct experience that can generate humility*. There are, of course, many others. I mention diversity because it came through in the CEOs I interviewed. What is important is that humility can form from strong personal experiences that are humbling.

Learning from Observation
Several CEOs described having parents who faced significant challenges. Although this was partly a direct experience because it affected the households in which

the interviewees grew up, it also served as an important way of learning indirectly from the experience of others. Parental struggles among my interviewees included immigration, disability, and modest economic backgrounds. Again, these are merely a subset of potential challenges that parents can face, and it's likely that difficulties faced by siblings or others who are quite close to us would have a similar effect. Yet the prevalence of this among the dozen people interviewed merits attention.

Howard Behar's and Phyllis Campbell's parents started and ran small businesses to provide for their families. Behar is a first-generation American; his parents were immigrants. English was not their native language, and they experienced the need for cultural adaptation after coming here. Phyllis Campbell's parents were second-generation Americans. Yet, as Japanese Americans, her grandparents and most of their children were confined in a Japanese internment camp during World War II; they lost the family's grocery store. Campbell's father ultimately found employment in a dry-cleaning store, which he was later able to own.

Brad Tilden's father had polio. In our discussion, his father seemed quite heroic. Yet it was evident that Tilden was humbled by observing the challenges his father faced every day.

In a similar way, modest economic circumstances contributed to humility. Campbell described expecting to work in her family's dry-cleaning store because her parents did not have the means for her to go to college until she received a scholarship at the last minute from an anonymous benefactor. Tilden mentioned growing up not far from Alaska Airlines' headquarters, an area of modest economic circumstances. He said that he knew mechanics at the airline who grew up in the same area and realized he could have taken the same path.

Seeing others struggle and being close to others of modest means seems to contribute to humility. It appears that part of our identity—of who we are—is shaped more humbly from these circumstances than it might be if struggle were not evident.

Social Beliefs and Norms

We all grow up in a context that includes social beliefs and norms. Interviewees reported their humility being formed by contexts such as regional norms, parental teaching, and religion/faith.

When it comes to regional norms for humility, the Midwest seems to stand out. Dick Johnson, Alan Mulally, and Jim Weber hail from the Midwest and spoke about how that regional culture discouraged arrogance. Instead, it encouraged hard work and respect for others' dignity.

Most interviewees also described how their parents taught them humility. Orlando Ashford, Phyllis Campbell, Roger Ferguson, Alan Mulally, Jeff Musser, and Jim Sinegal cited specific parental teachings or family values that helped them realize they were not above (or below) others. Howard Behar, Sally Jewell, and Brad Tilden provided examples of watching their parents and learning from their humble behavior.

Finally, interviewees cited religious upbringing or faith beliefs as part of their training in humility. Ashford, Mulally, and Noseworthy expressed strong influence from Christian teaching or church experiences.

Can Leader Humility Be Taught?

It is interesting to observe these themes among interviewees. Even though the sample was small, it's not hard to imagine how experiences of marginalization, observing parents' struggles, and social upbringing can encourage personal humility. A logical question is whether leader humility can be taught to those who may lack it.

The answer is partly yes. Humility requires self-awareness and free will (choice). If people have the right foundation (the elements being reasonable self-awareness and openness to growth in this), there is a good chance they can develop or improve leader humility. If one or the other element is lacking, the odds are not good.

Assuming the foundation is there, the themes found in the interviews are good indicators for how we can help adult leaders form humility: direct experience, observational learning, and values clarification. These tools take time—they do not fit well in a short course on leadership training. But they can be worked into longer, experiential formats—distributed over time—whether in organizational leadership programs or those led by universities or consultants.

That is precisely the type of formative work I have engaged in for many years. Credit-bearing executive programs at Seattle University provide working managers with a broad, contextual knowledge of the interrelatedness of social systems. Participants are concurrently challenged to meet and work in a leadership capacity with populations they are otherwise unlikely to meet. In the process, they shed stereotypes and develop empathy and a balanced, more inclusive, ego. They often reconsider their own privilege and become more intentional about the positive impact they want to have—not only at work but beyond. Consider this report from a former student when asked years later, as a senior leader, if the formative work we had done together made a difference:

A very broadening moment in my life was encounter-
ing Ed as I was delivering food for the Renton Food
Bank during our Social Justice Project. It was powerful
to learn that he had been a pilot like me and, like me,
was educated in Engineering at Seattle University, but
through very unfortunate circumstances had become
homeless. I realized then that all of our paths are frail
and that any set of unknowns could put any of us in
a very different place—something I would not have
imagined if I'd never encountered that population.
But this has been a big influence on how I think about
my family and my team's health. I now have a much
more sympathetic ear when it comes to taking care of
employees.

Now I also think about "How can I make the world
better?" One example involved taking relief supplies to
Chile after the earthquake there. I had a client whose
jet could be converted to a freighter, and I saw the
opportunity in a way I wouldn't have before. After getting permission to use the freighter for this purpose,
an amazing set of things aligned so that, in one week,
we flew 12.5 thousand pounds of relief supplies to
Santiago, where the plane was greeted by the Red Cross,
who unloaded and distributed the goods. That was very
gratifying, but it speaks to how much power we have
to lead from where we sit in ways that make a big difference. I was able to move a much bigger rock this way
than by simply sending a personal donation. This is the
challenge for all leaders: it is often an "adjacency"—the

power we have from our positions allows us to influence more broadly. —CAPTAIN STEVE TAYLOR, FORMER PRESIDENT, BOEING BUSINESS JETS

If leader humility means a tendency to feel and display deep regard for others' dignity, it is evident in this example. It's about how we think, what we think about, how we view others, how we view our relationship to others, and—importantly—the ways we act. It may be developed from the experiences of our upbringing. And as adults, when the student is willing, with the right experiences, humility can be taught and learned.

Personal Development for Humility

What if you had little experience to help you develop humility? Or if you feel you have humility but would like to strengthen and apply it better for leadership? Growth in humility requires increasing both self-awareness and exposure to certain kinds of experiences. It can also help to transfer this learning to the job. This section provides a brief assessment for you to conduct, sample exercises to do on your own, and some suggestions to help you transfer learning to work.

Self-Assessment

Leader humility is partly in the eye of the beholder. For this reason, our own view of our humility is incomplete, and we need to check in with others. In the quiz here (table 6), rate yourself and ask others how they might rate you. You might copy and share this with several people and ask them to return it anonymously, if you like. It helps to select at least a couple of people with whom your work relationship may not be ideal. People already have

TABLE 6. Leader Humility Check-In: *Leader humility means feeling and displaying a deep regard for others' dignity.*

HOW IS MY HUMILITY?		
TO WHAT EXTENT:	Self-rating (rate 1–5 with 5 being high)	Others' Rating (rate 1–5 with 5 being high)
Do I talk about myself too much?		
Am I known for doing the right thing?		
Do I include people in conversations and meetings about issues when it really matters to them?		
Do I dominate conversations, cutting others off?		
Have I shared a clear and compelling vision for our work that shows how it supports the greater good?		
Am I true to my word?		
Do I openly express genuine concern for all stakeholders?		
Do I listen? Am I open to ideas that are not my own?		
Do I demonstrate concern for others' long-term interests?		
Do I interact with everyone in respectful ways?		

an opinion of us, so we might as well know what it is. Pay attention to answers on individual questions. Take credit for what may be going well, and consider what may need to change.

Exercises

Among the interviewees, humility was often formed from experiences: growing up in the Midwest, having parents who faced challenges or stressed humility, absorbing faith influences, or having been marginalized in some way. Perhaps you had similar experiences—or not. This section can help you reflect on your background and shore up areas that may be needed.

1. Reflect on your life experiences. What were you taught about each of the following?

   a. Your superiority compared to others.

   b. Which types of people are lesser than you (such as women, minorities, the uneducated, immigrants). Consider messages from family and, more broadly, from the media.

   c. Whether human life itself is valuable.

2. If you answered yes to 1.c., but you believe you are superior to other groups of people in certain ways, can you modify your belief to hold that just as human life is valuable, everyone's *dignity* (sense of self-worth) is valuable? If so, consider that the personal component of their dignity needs to be honored just as we honor life itself.

3. Have you had a significant failure as a leader? Think it over and recall what went wrong. Were there stakeholders who contributed to your failure because you had neglected to include, engage, or represent them?

4. How homogeneous was your upbringing? Were you around people mainly like your-self or exposed to many different groups with wide-ranging perspectives and experiences?

5. If your background was homogeneous, make a genuine attempt to meet and talk personally

with five people, each from a unique background that is also very different from yours
(such as homeless, gender alternative, disabled,
veteran, low income, single parent). The point is
to learn something about them and understand
their experience and views. You might meet
such people through volunteering or through
community meetings. They can be found in
cafés and on the streets. Rather than walking
by people who are different from you, consider
acknowledging them and striking up a conversation when it is appropriate. This exercise can
be done over many months, but it can help you
understand others—and yourself—in new ways.

On the Job

Translating this reflection and exercise to work is important. Here are some considerations for improving your
interactions with people over the long haul.

- Is there someone you have avoided because you
  seem to have conflict—yet you know he or she
  is a stakeholder? Consider reaching out to that
  person or group to let them know you'd like to
  meet and explore how to collaborate. See if you
  can bring in a facilitator to the meeting. The
  goals should be to (1) show regard for the dignity of those with whom you are in conflict; (2)
  clarify behavioral norms on each side for working together well; and (3) identify a shared goal,
  or at least agree on parameters (the scope) for
  your working together.

- With whom do you find it hard to work? What is it about that person that is tough for you? Think about how you can interact to support that person's dignity—and ask for him or her to support yours.

- Review the self-assessment you took. Work to improve areas in which you received critical feedback. Consider sharing with your raters that you heard this feedback and are working to change. Ask their help in letting you know how you are doing, and check back if they don't volunteer that they see progress.

▶ IDEAS FOR ACTION

1. In the next two weeks, look for these opportunities to show a balanced ego as you interact with others:

   a. Show gratitude to five of your stakeholders. Make a point to thank them for something they do well. Email is fine, but a sincere, handwritten note is a personal touch that has a bigger impact.

   b. Admit to one or more stakeholders that you don't know something, and praise them for their knowledge about it and contribution to your collective work.

   c. If you are being criticized, listen carefully—without making excuses or seeming upset with the person delivering the message.

   d. Do you recall a time when you have upset someone by harming their dignity? Offer a sincere apology.

2. Consider how you can support the development of others:

   a. Look for moments when they share great ideas, take initiative, or perform exceptionally well. Take a moment to compliment them and learn more about their background, skill, or interest in it.

   b. Which of your stakeholders do you tend to ignore or neglect? Reach out and ask about their needs and goals.

   c. Is there someone who is clearly ready for more (a promotion or transfer to a more responsible position)? Can you advocate for him or her within your organization? If not, have a talk with that person about his or her interests. Examine your network for opportunities and referrals.

3. Make integrity a priority for working together:

   a. Tell the truth, even when it may not be favorable for you.

   b. Discourage shortcuts among your team when those actions are ethically inappropriate.

   c. As needed, advocate upward for policies and practices that are honest and match stated values.

Now let's take a look at the bios and personal experiences of the CEOs interviewed, listed in alphabetical order. As you consider them, note that having leader humility did not limit the heights they reached. Indeed, it supported their exceptional achievements.

Orlando Ashford

President of Holland America Line, Orlando Ashford leads the award-winning cruise line's brand and business, including its fleet of fourteen premium vessels that have carried more than nine hundred thousand guests annually to all seven continents. Previously, Ashford was president of the Talent Business Segment for Mercer, the global consulting leader in talent, health, retirement, and investments, following senior executive roles at Marsh & McLennan Companies, Motorola, and the Coca-Cola Company, where he also served as group director of human resources for ninety countries in Eurasia and Africa. Ashford was selected by *Seattle Business* magazine for the 2019 Executive Excellence Award; *Black Enterprise* magazine named Ashford to their 2017 list of the "Most Powerful Executives in Corporate America"; and, in 2016, he was named to *Savoy* magazine's list of "Top 100 Most Influential Blacks in Corporate America." Ashford serves on the advisory board of Purdue University School of Technology, the board of directors of ITT, and the Virginia Mason board of directors. He holds a Bachelor of Science degree and Master of Science degree in Organizational Leadership and Industrial Technology from Purdue University.

ON DEVELOPING HUMILITY: "This is just how I was raised. My parents, especially my Mom, emphasized humility. I remember my Mom saying, 'No one in this world is any better than you. And no one in this world is any worse than you.' I was taught to treat everyone according to the Golden Rule. I grew up in a Christian household with values on treating people as I would want to be treated."

Howard Behar

During his twenty-one years at Starbucks Coffee, Howard Behar led the domestic business, as president of North America, and was the founding president of Starbucks Coffee Company International. He participated in the growth of the company from twenty-eight stores to over fifteen thousand stores spanning five continents, with approximately three hundred thousand employees serving one hundred million people a week. He served on the Starbucks Board of Directors for twelve years before retiring and continues to serve on the boards of iD Tech, Education Elements, and Anthos Capital. In 2018, he received the "Lifetime Achievement Award" from *Seattle Business* magazine. He remains committed to the development and education of our future leaders and has been a longtime advocate of the servant leadership model. Behar has also authored two books on leadership, titled *It's Not About the Coffee* and *The Magic Cup*.

ON DEVELOPING HUMILITY: "My parents immigrated from Latvia and Bulgaria. They didn't speak the language at first, but they saved their pennies and opened a small grocery store with an apartment above for the five of us. My parents never had much, but we learned how to work. When I was young, I watched how Dad was kind and honest with his customers. One time he had me get two trays of strawberries for someone, and I noticed they didn't pay him when they left. I asked him about that, and he said not everything we do should be for pay. He understood that family was not doing so well. . . . I've never forgotten the way he showed them kindness. It wasn't about being liberal or conservative. It was about people helping people."

Phyllis Campbell

Phyllis Campbell is chairwoman of JPMorgan Chase, Pacific Northwest. Previously, she served as the president and CEO of the Seattle Foundation, the largest community foundation in Washington, whose charitable assets doubled to $600 million under her leadership. Earlier, Campbell served as CEO of U.S. Bank, becoming the first female CEO of a bank in Washington state. She is currently an independent director for Alaska Air Group, where she chairs the Nominating Committee, and was previously on the Nordstrom board of directors. She also serves on the Diversity Advisory Board of Toyota, is chairwoman of the board of the US-Japan Council, is a member of the global advisory board of Women Corporate Directors, and is a member of the National Association of Corporate Directors' Nominating and Governance Advisory Council. Campbell earned her BA at Washington State University and her executive MBA from the University of Washington.

ON DEVELOPING HUMILITY: "Humility is derived from my upbringing and Japanese American heritage. My father's family was interned in Idaho during World War II and lost the family grocery store. My father escaped internment by being sent to Spokane to finish high school. He enrolled in the US Army, to prove his loyalty to this country, in spite of his father, brother, and sisters being incarcerated. He later went back to Spokane, finding employment as a dry cleaner—one of the few jobs he could find. Over time, he owned the dry-cleaning business. We were always taught to focus on giving back to others, not calling attention to ourselves. In business and in the community, this trait has translated into paying attention to the good of the whole."

Roger Ferguson

Roger Ferguson is president and CEO (2008–present) of Teachers Insurance and Annuity Association (TIAA), a Fortune 100 financial-services organization with over $1 trillion in assets, serving employees across fifteen thousand institutions and fifty-five million individuals as the leading provider of financial services in the academic, research, medical, cultural, and governmental fields. He served as vice chairman of the Board of Governors of the US Federal Reserve System from 1999 to 2006 and today is chairman of the Conference Board, and a member of other boards, including those of Alphabet, General Mills, Memorial Sloan Kettering Cancer Center, and the Smithsonian Institution. A Fellow of the American Academy of Arts and Sciences, Ferguson earned his AB in economics, his JD, and his PhD in economics, all from Harvard University. He began his career as an attorney at Davis Polk & Wardwell and then joined McKinsey & Company, where he became partner.

ON DEVELOPING HUMILITY: "I grew up in Washington, DC. My mom was a schoolteacher and my dad was a cartographer in the Army. We lived behind Langston Terrace, the first public housing project in the country. I started my education at a segregated elementary school and then got into an honors program at an integrated junior high school that was a phenomenal melting pot. I later went to Harvard on a scholarship and took a work-study job cleaning bathrooms. I got plenty of practice in doing what my parents always taught me: no job is too small to do well. What drove me was an internal sense of pride, a joy of learning, and a recognition that academics was a way I could fit in."

Sally Jewell

Growing up in Washington state inspired Sally Jewell's love of the outdoors. Her early career as an engineer for Mobil led to helping Rainier Bank evaluate energy loans, which led to nearly twenty years' experience in the banking industry. In 1996, Jewell joined the board of directors for Recreational Equipment, Inc. (REI). In 2000 she was named COO; she became CEO in 2005, and she was named "CEO of the Year" by *Puget Sound Business Journal* in 2006. Jewell was nominated by President Obama and confirmed by the Senate in 2013 as secretary, US Department of the Interior, where she led the agency of seventy thousand employees that is responsible for nearly one-fifth of all land in the United States. Jewell has served on many boards, including those of Symetra, Premera, the Retail Industry Leaders Association, the Nature Conservancy, the University of Washington, the National Parks Conservation Association, and the Mountains to Sound Greenway Trust, which she helped found. She received her BS in mechanical engineering from the University of Washington.

ON DEVELOPING HUMILITY: "I witnessed my parents' behavior and learned early on that when you are willing to admit you don't know something and you ask for help, people are almost always willing to lend their experience. Volunteering also gave me insights that helped me understand the value of listening, the benefit of different perspectives, and the barriers people face. And I believe nature nourishes the soul. Exploring wilderness, paddling through the Salish Sea, enjoying a field of wildflowers, or standing on a mountaintop can help all of us recognize our insignificance and reinforce our humility."

Dick Johnson

Chairman (since 2016) and president and CEO (since 2014) of Foot Locker, Inc., Richard A. Johnson (also known as Dick) served in many distinguished roles in this leading global retailer of athletically inspired shoes and apparel. His roles have included service as chief operating officer and executive vice president of Foot Locker, Inc., and chief executive officer and president at Foot Locker Europe B.V., a subsidiary of Foot Locker, Inc. He has been a director of H&R Block, Inc., and Maidenform Brands. He has also served as a director of the Retail Industry Leaders Association and the Footwear Distributors and Retailers of America. Johnson is a graduate of the University of Wisconsin–Eau Claire.

ON DEVELOPING HUMILITY: "I grew up in Wisconsin. My father was a construction superintendent, and my mother worked to help support the family. Although my parents were from humble beginnings, they worked hard to get things done and always gave of themselves to their children and community." Asked how he came to view humility as essential to effective leadership, Johnson replied, "It's just the way I was brought up. Growing up, I learned this is just what you do. It was never, 'Hey, it's about me. I led X.' It just wasn't about me. From my first leadership role to being CEO of a company, I've realized it's not about me. It's about the people we are leading and the consumers we serve."

Alan Mulally

As president and CEO of the Ford Motor Company, Alan Mulally led Ford's transformation into one of the world's leading automobile companies and the number one automobile brand in the United States. Prior to joining Ford, he served as president and CEO of Boeing Commercial Airplanes and president of Boeing Information, Space and Defense Systems. Mulally has been named number three among "the World's 50 Greatest Leaders" by *Fortune,* one of "The World's Most Influential People" by *Time*, and one of the thirty "World's Best CEOs" by *Barron's*. He holds BS and MS degrees in aeronautical and astronautical engineering from the University of Kansas, and a master's in management from the Massachusetts Institute of Technology. Mulally serves on the boards of directors for Alphabet, Carbon 3D, and the Mayo Clinic. He is a member of the US National Academy of Engineering and a Fellow of England's Royal Academy of Engineering.

ON DEVELOPING HUMILITY: "Growing up in the Midwest, we lived with very modest means. My parents had a strong faith and believed that I could make a significant contribution to the greater good. My parents lived and taught me the following lessons about humility, love, and service that I have carried with me: the purpose of life is to love and be loved, in that order; to serve is to live; seek to understand before seeking to be understood; it's nice to be important, but more important to be nice; by working together with others, you can make the most positive contribution to the most people; lifelong learning and continuous improvement; respect and include everyone—we are all creatures of God and worthy to be loved; develop one integrated life to deliver your life's work."

Jeff Musser

Jeff Musser has been president and CEO of Expeditors International since December 2013. He began his career as a part-time messenger with Expeditors in 1983 and spent twenty-two years in progressively responsible roles in field operations and brokerage, including the roles of district manager and regional vice president. He later served as executive vice president and chief information officer, rounding out his broad and seasoned leadership profile. He is a licensed US Customs broker and holds an IATA/FIATA Certificate. Musser's unique portfolio consists of both field and global corporate leadership responsibilities, along with the increasingly critical information technology discipline. He is exceptionally well-qualified to lead Expeditors, valuing and reinforcing its unique culture for ongoing success.

ON DEVELOPING HUMILITY: "I grew up in a middle-class family with two amazing parents and three siblings. My father worked full-time as a police officer and helped supplement income by also working as a mechanic. My mother did the difficult job of raising three children while also providing childcare services. In our family, there was never a sense of entitlement and instead a focus on working hard and accepting the results of our efforts. We never judged those that had more, nor did we judge those that had less. We were encouraged to do the best we could in life with the tools we possessed but to also understand and respect that success is different to each individual. This created a strong conviction that serving others was paramount to the things that I wanted to achieve in life."

John Noseworthy, MD

John Noseworthy served as president and CEO of the Mayo Clinic from 2009 to 2018. Prior to that, he served as chair of the Mayo Clinic's Department of Neurology and medical director of the Department of Development. He received his MD from Dalhousie University and completed residencies and research fellowships in neurology and neuroimmunology at Dalhousie University, the University of Western Ontario, and Harvard Medical School. He holds certification in the Royal College of Physicians and Surgeons of Canada. He specialized in multiple sclerosis and spent more than two decades designing and conducting controlled clinical trials. He served as editor in chief of *Neurology* from 2007 to 2009. He served on the Board of Directors for Merck & Company, Inc., from 2017 to 2019 and was a health governor of the World Economic Forum from 2014 to 2018. He joined the Board of Directors of UnitedHealth Group and AlixPartners in 2019. He has received honorary doctorates from the University of Western Ontario and Dalhousie University and was named an Officer of the Order of the Orange-Nassau in 2014.

ON DEVELOPING HUMILITY: "My parents were very influential. My Dad was an Anglican Episcopal minister, and my Mom had deep religious beliefs. Humility was part of their faith and was passed along to me. My father helped me realize that if I were going to be successful, I needed to realize my limitations too. Later, from my profession of neurology, I've seen the courage of patients and families in dealing with complex, confusing, and often tragic illnesses. As a care provider, one realizes the human limitations we have, and that builds humility."

Jim Sinegal

Jim Sinegal is the cofounder and former chief executive officer of Costco Wholesale. He retired from the executive position in 2012 and remained a board director until 2018. Sinegal began his career in retail business as a college student, working for the legendary retail icon Sol Price at the discount store FedMart in San Diego. He later struck out on his own to start Costco with his business partner, Jeff Brotman. Costco today has revenues of more than $149 billion and operates 783 warehouses in forty-four states, Puerto Rico, and thirteen countries. The company employs more than 254,000 people worldwide and has earned the reputation as a fair and progressive employer. Sinegal has been named one of *Bloomberg Businessweek's* "Best Managers," one of the "30 Most Respected CEOs" by *Barron's* from 2006 to 2011, one of the "100 Most Influential People" by *Time*, and *Morningstar Investments'* "Outstanding CEO of the Year" in 2011. He serves as trustee for Fred Hutchinson Cancer Research Center and has served as executive in residence or adviser at Seattle University, San Diego State University, and University of Notre Dame. He earned his AA from San Diego College and a BA from San Diego State University.

ON DEVELOPING HUMILITY: "Raised in Pittsburgh, in a working-class Catholic family, I learned important values about how you treat people." Criticized by some investors for being too generous to employees, he told James Flanigan of the *Los Angeles Times* (Flanigan 2004), "I don't see what's wrong with an employee earning enough to be able to buy a house or have a health plan for the family. We're trying to build a company that will be here 50 years from now."

Brad Tilden

Brad Tilden is chairman, president, and CEO of Alaska Air Group and its two subsidiaries, Alaska Airlines, the fifth-largest US airline, and Horizon Air, its regional affiliate. After his early career in accounting at Price Waterhouse, Tilden joined Alaska Airlines in 1991, later serving as Alaska Air Group's chief financial officer and president before being named chief executive officer in 2012. Tilden was named Executive of the Year in 2015 by the *Puget Sound Business Journal* and among the "Top 50 Corporate Leaders in America" in 2016 by *Fortune* magazine. Alaska Air Group is a leader in sustainability and has held the J.D. Power "Highest in Customer Satisfaction Among Traditional Carriers in North America" award since 2008. Tilden earned his BA from Pacific Lutheran University and executive MBA from the University of Washington.

ON DEVELOPING HUMILITY: "My values around humility came from my father especially. He was one of the last people to get polio. He got it in the '50s when he was 19 or 20 years old. He spent the majority of his life on crutches or in a wheelchair, but I think polio caused him to dig deep, and he had a very successful career at Boeing, and he and my Mom raised a fantastic family of 6 kids. My Dad was a quiet, humble man. He was funny, kind, and gentle. He wasn't a 'victim'—and was not bitter. In fact, he didn't talk about the polio. There was zero self-pity. He just had humility and worked hard to make his life work. It was the example I saw every day growing up."

Jim Weber

Jim Weber has been president and CEO of Brooks Running since 2001, a subsidiary of Berkshire Hathaway that designs and markets high-performance men's and women's running shoes, clothing, and accessories. After an early career at Wells Fargo and then Pillsbury (now part of General Mills), Weber became president of a division of Coleman at age thirty. He later served as president of O'Brien International, then became CEO of Sims Sports. In 1999, he joined Piper Jaffray Investment Bank as well as the Board of Directors of Brooks. Weber was named "Entrepreneur of the Year" in the Pacific Northwest region by Ernst & Young in 2013; was named one of the nine most influential innovators in the running industry by *Runner's World* magazine in 2015; and has been on the "Power 100" list, the most influential people in the footwear industry, for the past ten years. Weber earned a BS from the University of Minnesota and an MBA at Dartmouth's Tuck School of Business.

ON DEVELOPING HUMILITY: "Part of it was growing up in Minnesota. It is a hardworking, self-reliant, carry your own weight culture, but it's not a podium culture. Arrogance, grandstanding, and selfishness are discouraged. In Midwest farming communities, a self-reliance meshed with helping your neighbor has shaped environments where selfishness creates isolation. As well, I found Midwesterners approachable, and my early bosses were extremely generous in coaching me. Many companies gave back 5 percent of their profits annually to the community, and this instilled in me a sense to give back—it's just part of what you do."

CHAPTER TEN

Extraordinary Power—for Business and Beyond

There is no respect for others without humility in oneself.
—Henri Frederic Amiel

The twelve CEOs interviewed for this book provide excellent insights into the value of humility in leadership. They have all attained great heights professionally, yet they retain a personal humility that displays deep regard for others' dignity. Let's now return to why and how humility is an *extraordinary* power for leaders in business, as well as in so many other endeavors.

It is my belief that the exceptional achievements of the CEOs I interviewed were fueled not only by hard work and knowledge, but by their personal humility. I believe this because of Collins's (2001) research and because I have heard hundreds of enthusiastic and unsolicited stories from people who worked with leaders who displayed regard for others' dignity. Let me share just one comment that is typical of the way in which a leader's humility affects other people:

My colleague and I were honored to receive an invitation to Sally Jewell's swearing-in ceremony at the White House for her appointme nt as secretary, US Department of the Interior, under President Obama. Sally had invited us out a day early, and on arrival to the Department of the Interior we were delighted to see Sally's new photograph, framed and hanging right below President Obama's on the wall. As we whipped out our cameras to take a photo, we were immediately surrounded by the building security team, not because we were a threat, but because they wanted to know how we knew her, since she had only arrived a few weeks earlier. The security guard informed me that he had served at this post for 20+ years and had never met the likes of Madam Secretary Jewell. He told us that on her first day, she came into the building lugging her two large suitcases, wearing running shoes . . . no car service, no taxi . . . she had ridden the subway with suitcases in tow. He went on to say she dropped her bags, introduced herself to all the staff, and wanted to know their names and how long they had worked there. He added, "That's not even the strangest thing! Do you know she comes down to the entrance of the building to greet people coming into the building in the morning? She walks everywhere, always on the go." But what was most impressive to this employee was that by week two, Sally not only knew his name, she knew about his wife, children, and grandchildren . . . also by name. "*Never*, he said, had anyone ever asked him such things, let alone made him feel like a part of the team." He was excited to work with her, offering her the best service he could. And he wanted to know all about her and if they could expect this type of connection throughout her service. We could confidently state that this is the Sally we have

known as a CEO, community leader, friend, and partner throughout our entire time serving with her, over a decade, and he and others would be in for other great surprises due to her humble and selfless leadership.
—MICHELLE CLEMENTS, FORMER SENIOR VICE PRESIDENT FOR REI

This example shows how profound people's reactions often are when they meet and work for leaders with humility. In a short time in office, followers had sized up Sally Jewell as humble. And this report shows how her behavior increased others' attention, drew them in and helped them appreciate her, and made them want to give their best. Let's revisit the model of six keys to leader humility (shown earlier in figure 5) and place the description of Sally Jewell's behaviors among its keys to leader humility.

Recall that people have three main questions about leaders. And they observe carefully for information that satisfies these three questions:

- Who Are You?

- Where Are We Going?

- Do You See Me?

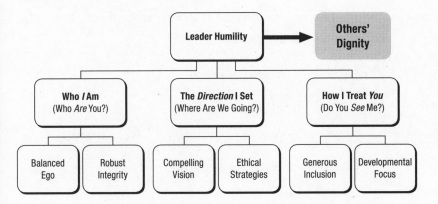

In the model of six keys to leader humility, we see clearly that people's early observations of Jewell focused on "Who Are You" and "Do You See Me?" They assessed her *behavior* in forming their own judgments about her. In this case, her taking the subway and carrying her own bags, eschewing the perks of her office, signaled a balanced ego. She also practiced generous inclusion by investing in getting to know people, thus making them feel seen. The early impressions formed about her were remarkable. They excited and galvanized her staff, who now felt part of a team. Notice that this example occurred *outside* of business: it is drawn from her service as a senior government official in her Cabinet position under President Obama. Human nature exists in all human contexts.

Leader humility matters because people work together best when their hearts and minds are engaged. As described in chapter 8, it takes personal humility coupled with strong drive to be a Total Leader, and it takes Total Leaders to create thriving organizations and great results. In businesses, the desirable outcomes generated by Total Leaders include the following:

- Strong financial performance

- Positive reputations for the organization's products and services

- Excellent customer relations

- Healthy workplace cultures

- Higher employee satisfaction and lower turnover

- Continuous learning and improvement

On the other hand, leaders who have strong drive but lack personal humility can be toxic to others. And toxic leaders create toxic organizations that fail to live up to their potential. Sadly, a great many leaders and organizations are toxic, as reported by people who work for them. I have heard many unsolicited comments from professional students over the years, many of them leaders themselves, about the toxicity of their work environments. I've heard similar comments about toxic leaders from inside other organizations when I have consulted. And the data on turnover and employee *dis*-engagement are rather compelling.

So, it is time to truly reexamine our ideas about strong leadership. Dominance, command, and control do have a place. In the words of Howard Behar, "When the building is on fire, you don't call a meeting to discuss what to do. You just tell people." But despite all of our deadlines and pressures, relatively few work situations qualify as a life-threatening emergency. Leaders who lack humility tend to focus on winning or dominating others (often ignoring the harm they cause in the process) or on gaining perks and status for themselves. This behavior is toxic because it violates the dignity of others. It results in lower trust, collaboration, and performance.

Although this book emphasizes business leadership, it includes interviews with CEOs of nonprofit and governmental organizations, as well as CEOs who serve as board members on nonprofit and governmental organizations. Actually, the principles of human dignity and leader humility apply to leaders in most contexts (for example, parents, educators, medical professionals, religious leaders, and athletic coaches). Yet the need for strong leadership in governmental and nonprofit organizations, as well as in civil society, is now imperative.

We are at an inflection point in history that demands leader humility for the health and progress of civilization. We face multiple, complex, and serious challenges. Resolving them effectively will necessitate leaders working together across business, government, and civil society. These are a few of our most evident problems:

- **Global health.** Geographic boundaries can no longer maintain the separation they once did. The COVID-19 pandemic showed that we are one planet, one people, and that society as we know it can quickly be brought to a standstill. Global health is intricately connected with global economic stability, and we need to collaborate on solutions for all. This will require diagnostic, containment, and therapeutic strategies, as well as improved communication.

- **Climate change.** Despite the presence of strong science and strong disbelief in science, global temperatures have been rising. Weather patterns have become more extreme. People and wildlife are being displaced through fires, rising sea levels, and damage to agriculture. We risk permanent damage to the planet that supports our existence—and that of future generations.

- **Migration/immigration.** Globally, the West has a crisis in immigration. This has led to political tensions in Europe and the United States as millions of people seek escape from societies with low opportunity and high violence. Many argue that we cannot take them all in; it is equally clear that we can't build enough walls to keep them all out.

- **International business.** Jobs, supplies, goods, and services also migrate around the world. This presents opportunities by providing broader markets and suppliers for businesses and less expensive goods for consumers. It also creates challenges: many workers have been displaced, and different laws and practices across countries have created numerous equity and ethical concerns. These are two sides of the same coin.

- **Wealth disparity.** The distribution of wealth has become quite distorted in the past few decades. Not only are some countries wealthier than others, but, increasingly, a small minority of people in the world hold vast quantities of wealth. This significantly constrains opportunity and quality of life for masses of people. Extreme wealth disparity is already creating political instability.

- **Mass information/disinformation.** The internet has transformed the way we share and gain information. As with many technological advances, its benefits are great, and it has a downside. We are witnessing the spread of misinformation to such an extent that it is hard to get agreement on what is true. Although abuse of internet platforms is widespread, there has been little effective resolution.

These and challenges of race and social injustice are exerting a powerful downward pull on developed societies, and our future will be greatly affected by how well we address them. People's views are widely polarized—not merely intellectually, but emotionally—because we do not agree on what is fact or truth. And when we cannot agree on what is true, policy formation is thwarted. Unfortunately, our opinions have become so divided that resolving them will be difficult. Yet, that is exactly why we need leaders—those whose job it is to hold themselves and the team collectively responsible and accountable for generating compelling visions, comprehensive strategies, and relentless implementation—for the greater good of all they serve.

Collectively, we are as responsible as ever for creating healthy communities. We need leaders who can represent—and integrate—the interests of *all*. More than ever, leaders need to help us find the principled, moral direction around which most people can rally. As Martin Luther King Jr. said, "A genuine leader is not a searcher for consensus but a molder of consensus."

Molding consensus, influencing others, galvanizing people to follow—these are all central to the work of leadership. By contrast, trying to win an outcome by force invites backlash because win-lose approaches create losers. And since everyone (including those who are forced to lose today) has and needs a sense of self-worth—a sense of dignity—those who lose today will seek to retaliate or gain tomorrow. It is time for leaders to honor the dignity of all people. That begins by recognizing all of our stakeholders and working together with them toward shared goals.

Does this mean that we can always expect enthusiastic support from the opposition? Or from poor performers? Certainly it does not. But few situations are so extreme as to justify violating human dignity when dealing with opposition and poor performance. Because most people want genuine progress, supporting the dignity of others, even while holding to strong standards, is likely to increase collaboration and progress in most situations.

And while we may not be able to please everyone, we can make a serious effort. Coalitions can be formed across divergent groups to develop vision and goals that serve the broader good. These visions and goals can then be communicated widely, along with the rationale behind them. Constituents should be invited frequently to comment, and there will need to be give and take: the initial vision may need to broaden and goals may need to be adjusted. However, our complex challenges can be resolved only when leaders shift from seeking short-term wins to finding long-term solutions that address the needs and concerns of most stakeholders. This enables the greatest support for implementation and genuine progress on issues that are important to so many of us.

As we become more educated, affluent, and sophisticated, we may underestimate the importance of traditional values. Yet ideas favoring honorable character and a strong moral compass are timeless in their wisdom. We are social creatures living in community, both local and global, so our attitudes and behavior have a significant impact on others. And social impact is amplified among those with power—leaders. We entrust leaders to provide direction, but we expect to be seen and cared for in return. Leaders need to honor the dignity of all people by showing good character (balanced ego and integrity), setting healthy vision and strategy, and demonstrating that others are seen by providing genuine inclusion and opportunities for progress that supports others' needs and interests.

Having strong drive and even being right, while helpful in leadership, are not enough. If we fail to maintain healthy relationships with stakeholders, results are not optimal. Molding consensus requires us to ask if we have proposed a direction that others feel they can accept. Getting there takes humility because we have to step back and ask, "Who are all my stakeholders, and am I addressing their needs?"

> *Coming together is a beginning,*
> *Staying together is progress,*
> *And working together is success.*
>
> —Henry Ford

I hope this book will be a call to action for leaders in business—and beyond. I urge you to pause and ask this question of yourself in the broadest sense: **Who are the people I must serve?** That is a different question—and likely a more challenging responsibility—than determining: How can I win for my team?

As modeled by the leaders interviewed for this book, we must serve *all* our stakeholders. We need to use a wide-angle lens to see who is affected by our work, invite them into our discussions, listen to their views, engage them in working together with us, and guide our progress toward mutual agreement. This can be hard and messy work—but it is the work of leadership—in all sectors.

It is the work the public wants to see accomplished by elected officials. It's the work we want done across business, government, and civil society to address our deep social challenges. And, of course, it is the work we ask of corporations that draw so heavily on our time and talents throughout most of our lives, while also providing the goods and services we need and want—and trust to be wholesome for us.

In fact, leadership, in all sectors, reflects trust that is placed in some individuals for the benefit of others. It is a form of high, almost sacred, trust that should not be violated. Leader humility keeps this trust alive by helping us avoid self-serving behaviors. It does this by keeping at the top of our minds that dignity matters for all of our stakeholders.

Leader humility extends to others a form of love—love for the life and nobility of those beyond oneself. And humility is extraordinarily powerful precisely because love earns the greatest commitment from stakeholders in our work.

Someday, after mastering the winds,
the waves, the tides and gravity,

we shall harness for God the energies of love,

and then, for the second time in the history of the world,
man will have discovered fire.

—Pierre Teilhard de Chardin

Discussion Guide

This guide provides suggestions for group discussion and learning. It is appropriate for use in work teams, courses on leadership, and workshops on leadership development.

Work Teams

1. How well are we working together?

2. Do we all truly show deep regard for others' dignity?

3. Are we guilty of telling jokes at others' expense?

4. Does our vision and strategy support the greater good for all our stakeholders?

5. Do we measure that?

Courses and Workshops

1. The concept of servant leadership (Greenleaf 1977) remains popular today. Is leader humility important for being a servant leader? If so, how?

2. How common is humility among leaders? What evidence do you see that supports your view?

3. Can leaders be effective without showing humility? Is the impact different?

4. Are there certain situations in which leader humility is inappropriate?

5. Why should leaders define their stakeholder groups broadly? What happens when they do not?

6. Do we need leaders who care to bring people together for the greater good? How can they do this?

7. How do you decide whether to keep someone who has low regard for others' dignity but is a top performer? What is the risk of keeping such a person as an employee (if he or she won't change)? What about the risk of keeping that person in a leadership role?

8. How important is it for leaders to ensure that people work together well?

9. Isn't it appropriate to retain well-developed employees? Why would you want to consider supporting their further development if that could help them leave?

10. Do you believe that everyone needs a sense of self-worth?

11. Is it appropriate that people get to define what about themselves is worthy?

12. Can we really honor others' dignity while disagreeing with (and taking action to correct) their behavior?

13. How do leader displays of anger and hostility affect others' dignity?

14. How does social media's "cancel culture" (unfollowing, thumbs-down in dislike, anonymous bullying) affect the norms of how we treat people in the workplace?

15. What is the compelling vision you share with others about your work?

16. Is there evidence that leaders behave unethically? Do you believe this is frequent?

17. With competing pressures, where should leaders draw the line about ethical behavior?

18. What societal problems would benefit from leaders working together?

19. Do you think leader humility is appropriate in the political environment? Why or why not?

20. What can you do as a leader to be a force for improving your organization's culture?

References

Beer, Jeff. 2019. "One Year Later, What Did We Learn from Nike's Blockbuster Colin Kaepernick Ad?" *Fast Company.* September 5, 2019. https://www.fastcompany.com/90399316/one-year-later-what-did-we-learn-from-nikes-blockbuster-colin-kaepernick-ad

Bonzanno, John. 2018. "Google Exits Pentagon (JEDI) Project after Employee Protests." *Observer.* October 10, 2018. https://observer.com/2018/10/google-pentagon-jedi/

Business Roundtable. 2019. "Business Roundtable Redefines the Purpose of a Corporation to Promote 'An Economy that Serves All Americans.'" August 19, 2019. https://www.businessroundtable.org/business-roundtable-redefines-the-purpose-of-a-corporation-to-promote-an-economy-that-serves-all-americans

Castle, Regan. 2018. "The Top 5 Challenges Faced by Business Executives." *Forbes* Councils. October 15, 2018. https://forbescouncils.com/2018/10/top-5-executive-challenges/

Catalyst. 2018. "Turnover and Retention: Quick Take." May 23, 2018. https://www.catalyst.org/research/turnover-and-retention/

Collins, Jim. 2001. *Good to Great: Why Some Companies Make the Leap . . . and Others Don't.* New York: HarperCollins Publishers, Inc.

Collins, Jim. 2005. "Level 5 Leadership: The Triumph of Humility and Fierce Resolve." *Harvard Business Review.* July–August.

Davis, Todd. 2018. "Humility: Lifting Nearly Every Other Important Virtue to Greater Heights." *Community.* Thrive Global. September 20, 2018. https://thriveglobal.com/stories/humility/

Donnelly, Grace. 2018. "The Number of Black CEOs at Fortune 500 Companies Is at Its Lowest Since 2002." *Fortune.* February 28, 2018. https://fortune.com/2018/02/28/black-history-month-black-ceos-fortune-500/

Flanigan, James. 2004. "Costco Sees Value in Higher Pay." *Los Angeles Times.* February 15, 2004. https://www.latimes.com/archives/la-xpm-2004-feb-15-fi-flan15-story.html

Fortune. 2014. "The World's 50 Greatest Leaders (2014)." March 20, 2014. https://fortune.com/2014/03/20/worlds-50-greatest-leaders/

Greenleaf, Robert K. 1977. *Servant Leadership: A Journey into the Nature of Legitimate Power and Greatness.* New York: Paulist Press.

Hahn, Jason Duaine. 2019. "CEO Dan Price, Who Surprised Employees with a $70K Minimum Salary, Feels 'Relieved and Proud.'" *People.* November 7, 2019. https://people.com/human-interest/ceo-dan-price-raises-salary-70k-it-feels-right/

Harter, Jim. 2018. "Employee Engagement on the Rise in the U.S." Gallup. August 26, 2018. https://news.gallup.com/poll/241649/employee-engagement-rise.aspx

Hembree, Diana. 2018. "CEO Pay Skyrockets to 361 Times That of the Average Worker." *Forbes.* May 22, 2018. https://www.forbes.com/sites/dianahembree/2018/05/22/ceo-pay-skyrockets-to-361-times-that-of-the-average-worker/#50abcce0776d

Hess, Edward D., and Katherine Ludwig. 2017. *Humility Is the New Smart: Rethinking Human Excellence in the Smart Machine Age.* Oakland, CA: Berrett-Koehler Publishers.

Hicks, Donna. 2019. *Leading with Dignity: How to Create a Culture That Brings Out the Best in People.* New Haven: Yale University Press.

Hoffman, Bryce G. 2012. *American Icon: Alan Mulally and the Fight to Save Ford Motor Company.* New York: Crown Business.

Hunnicutt, Trevor. 2019. "Twitter Bans Political Ads; Facebook's Zuckerberg Defends Them." Reuters. October 30, 2019. https://www.reuters.com/article/us-twitter-ads/twitter-to-ban-political-ads-in-apparent-swipe-at-facebook-idUSKBN1X92IK

Investopedia. n.d. "Environmental, Social, and Governance (ESG) Criteria." James Chen; reviewed by Gordon Scott. Updated February 25, 2020. https://www.investopedia.com/terms/e/environmental-social-and-governance-esg-criteria.asp

Johnson, Kevin. 2018. "Starbucks CEO: Reprehensible Outcome in Philadelphia Incident." Starbucks. April 15, 2018. https://stories.starbucks.com/stories/2018/starbucks-ceo-reprehensible-outcome-in-philadelphia-incident

Knoepfel, Ivo. 2004. "Who Cares Wins: Connecting Financial Markets to a Changing World." UN Environment Programme. https://www.unepfi.org/fileadmin/events/2004/stocks/who_cares_wins_global_compact_2004.pdf

McKinsey & Company. 2017. "Attracting and Retaining the Right Talent." *Our Insights.* November 2017. https://www.mckinsey.com/business-functions/organization/our-insights/attracting-and-retaining-the-right-talent

Mehrabian, Albert. 1972. *Nonverbal Communication.* New Brunswick, NJ: Aldine Transaction.

Morris, J. Andrew, Céleste M. Brotheridge, and John C. Urbanski. 2005. "Bringing Humility to Leadership: Antecedents and Consequences of Leader Humility." *Human Relations* 58, issue 10: 1323–50.

Nielsen, Rob, and Jennifer A. Marrone. 2018. "Humility: Our Current Understanding of the Construct and Its Role in Organizations." *International Journal of Management Reviews.* January 2018.

Nielsen, Rob, Jennifer A. Marrone, and Holly S. Ferraro. 2014. *Leading with Humility.* New York: Routledge.

NPR. 2018. "Starbucks Closes More Than 8,000 Stores Today for Racial Bias Training." May 29, 2018. https://www.npr.org/sections/thetwo-way/2018/05/29/615119351/starbucks-closes-more-than-8-000-stores-today-for-racial-bias-training

Peltz, James F. 2019. "Jeff Bezos Expanded Amazon's Climate Change Pledge. His Workers Want More." *Los Angeles Times*. September 20, 2019. https://www.latimes.com/business/story/2019-09-19/amazon-climate-change

Ou, Amy Y., Anne S. Tsui, Angelo J. Kinicki, David A. Waldman, Zhixing Xiao, and Lynda Jiwen Song. 2014. "Humble Chief Executive Officers' Connections to Top Management Team Integration and Middle Managers' Responses." *Administrative Science Quarterly* 59: 34–72.

Schein, Edgar H., and Peter A. Schein. 2018. *Humble Leadership: The Power of Relationships, Openness, and Trust.* Oakland, CA: Berrett-Koehler Publishing.

Sears, Lindsay. 2017. "2017 Retention Report: Trends, Reasons, and Recommendations." Work Institute. https://cdn2.hubspot.net/hubfs/478187/2017%20Retention%20Report%20Campaign/Work%20Institute%202017%20-Retention%20Report.pdf

Tornoe, Rob. 2018. "What Happened at Starbucks in Philadelphia?" *Philadelphia Inquirer.* April 16, 2018. https://www.inquirer.com/philly/news/starbucks-philadelphia-arrests-black-men-video-viral-protests-background-20180416.html

Zillman, Claire. 2019. "The Fortune 500 Has More Female CEOs Than Ever Before." *Fortune.* May 16, 2019. https://fortune.com/2019/05/16/fortune-500-female-ceos/

Acknowledgments

This project could not have succeeded without the help of many people. I'd like to begin by thanking Father Pat O'Leary, S.J. for helping me discern that my insights on humility needed to be shared more widely and that writing this book was on my path. Our many conversations added to my vision and voice.

It is with tremendous gratitude and deep regard that I acknowledge the twelve CEOs interviewed for this book: Orlando Ashford, Howard Behar, Phyllis Campbell, Roger Ferguson, Sally Jewell, Dick Johnson, Alan Mulally, Jeff Musser, John Noseworthy, Jim Sinegal, Brad Tilden, and Jim Weber. All of you, including those of you who did not know me, were gracious with your time. I appreciate your candor in answering my questions, and I feel honored that you gave me freedom in how I used your material. Your insights combined with the book's narrative create a much richer story.

I owe profound thanks to Alan Mulally, who not only agreed to an interview and wrote the foreword but provided the chapter on the Working Together Management System. I cannot envision this book without illustrating your system to show how leader humility can work in practice. I am equally grateful for your support and collaboration over the years. Our work together provided significant inspiration for this project.

Sharon Parks and Geoff Bellman deserve sincere thanks for referring me to Berrett-Koehler. Our conversations helped me find the perfect publisher for this work.

And my very deep appreciation goes to Steve Piersanti, founder and former CEO of BK, for believing in this project at an early stage. As my editor, you somehow knew the right questions to ask me—at the right time—always modeling leader humility. You challenged me to craft my ideas in more compelling ways, resulting in a much better book. I trust you recognize your influence on this work.

Several reviewers were privy to earlier versions of the full manuscript and offered constructive feedback: Cindy Hamra, Lori Homer, Jeff Kulick, Admiral Chuck Larkin (Ret.), Mike McNair, Kerry Radcliffe, Quinetta Roberson, and Lorri Sheffer. I appreciate your observations, which, in aggregate, helped me improve my work. I am also grateful to family, friends, colleagues, clients, and students. Thank you so much for your ideas, encouragement, and support over the longer haul. And I hope the book makes you feel your investment was worthwhile.

In trying to acknowledge some, I have no doubt overlooked others and apologize here for any oversight. Let me close by thanking all those at Berrett-Koehler and affiliates who support the publication and dissemination of this book. Your kindness and collaboration mean the world to me.

Index

About the Authors

Marilyn Gist, PhD
(https://www.marilyngist.com)
With strong leadership experience and deep academic credentials, Marilyn has long been fascinated by the quality of relationships that leaders must form to influence others effectively. As a consultant, she has guided numerous organizations and CEOs to greater success. As a speaker, she has clarified the essential behaviors that generate loyal and high-impact teams. And as an educator, she has inspired students to adopt a growth mindset and become exceptional leaders.

By watching what works—and does not work—Gist became keenly aware that we don't gain followers by stepping on others' dignity. Over time, she has seen major changes in the expectations of leaders that employees, peers, competitors, customers, and diverse stakeholders have. Yet, she has been dismayed that our older models of leadership continue to influence how new and continuing leaders behave. The evidence is strong that arrogant, command-and-control approaches yield limited results. This led her to develop and offer the approach in this book. Based on leader humility, this approach is simple to understand and learn in order to create thriving organizations and great results.

Leader humility is not meekness or weakness. It is simply a tendency to feel and display a deep regard for others' dignity. Marilyn found, both in her own work as a leader and in her mentoring of others, that leader humility has profound results. To amplify this message, she interviewed the twelve CEOs in this book, and invited the chapter written by Alan Mulally, to add *their* advice and experiences to her own voice. These individuals, currently or in the past, have led organizations as renowned as Alaska Airlines, Brooks Running, Costco, Expeditors International, Foot Locker, Ford Motor Company, Holland America, JPMorgan Chase Northwest, the Mayo Clinic, REI, Starbucks, TIAA, and the US Department of the Interior. Their great success shows how humility can make a difference for leaders everywhere.

Dr. Gist's work in leadership development began through the Center for Creative Leadership and continued in professorships at the University of North Carolina at Chapel Hill and the University of Washington. At UW, she held the Boeing Endowed Professorship of Business Management and served as faculty director of executive MBA programs. Most recently, Marilyn led Seattle University's Leadership EMBA degree program (anchored in a model of leader humility) from its inception in 2006 to rank as high as number eleven in the nation by *U.S. News & World Report*. She served as executive director of the Center for Leadership Formation, and associate dean and professor of management, at the Albers School of Business and Economics. In 2017, she received the Distinguished Faculty Award from the Alumni Board of

Governors and, in 2019, was named professor emerita by Seattle University's president.

Marilyn earned her BA from Howard University and her MBA and PhD from the University of Maryland, College Park. Her scholarly work has received more than twelve thousand citations in the published work of others, demonstrating exceptional thought leadership and visibility. Dr. Gist is a member of the Academy of Management, the American Psychological Association, and the International Women's Forum.

Alan Mulally

One of the world's best leaders, Alan has been ranked number three on *Fortune*'s "The World's 50 Greatest Leaders," one of the thirty "World's Best CEOs" by *Barron's*, one of "The World's Most Influential People" by *Time*, and "Chief Executive of the Year" by *Chief Executive* magazine. These honors flowed from his career contributions, industry leadership, and service.

Mr. Mulally served as president and chief executive officer of the Ford Motor Company and as a member of Ford's board of directors from September 2006 to June 2014. During this time, he led Ford's transformation into one of the world's leading automobile companies and the number one automobile brand in the United States. He guided Ford in working together on a compelling vision, comprehensive strategy, and implementation of the One Ford plan to deliver profitable growth for all of the company's stakeholders. He also was honored with the American Society for Quality's medal for excellence in executive leadership, the Automotive Executive of the Year designation, and the Thomas Edison Achievement Award.

Prior to joining Ford, Mulally had a long and distinguished career in aerospace. He served as executive vice president of the Boeing Company, president and CEO of Boeing Commercial Airplanes, and president of Boeing Information, Space and Defense Systems.

Equally impressive is that Alan has been deeply committed to helping others grow and succeed in leadership. He speaks and consults widely on the approach he developed: the Working Together Management System. For the first time, Alan has authored a chapter to share this approach. He explains in detail the operational process and Expected Behaviors involved in Working Together that you can follow to success. He shows how WTMS is deeply anchored in leader humility—and explains why humility is essential for making it work. Alan's own life, based on humility, love, and service, has earned him many followers and fans.

In addition to consulting and speaking, Alan is currently very active on boards of directors: Alphabet (parent company of Google), Carbon 3D, and the Mayo Clinic. These reflect areas where he brings his deep experience in engineering and business leadership to the future of design and manufacturing, information technology, sustainability, and health sciences.

Alan's past service includes being president of the American Institute of Aeronautics and Astronautics and chairman of the Board of Governors of the Aerospace Industries Association. He also served on President Obama's United States Export Council; as cochairman of the Council on Competitiveness in Washington, DC; and on the advisory boards of the National Aeronautics and Space Administration, the University of Washington, the University of Kansas, the Massachusetts Institute of Technology, and the United States Air Force Scientific Advisory Board. He is a member of the United States National Academy of Engineering and a fellow of England's Royal Academy of Engineering.

Mulally holds bachelor's and master of science degrees in aeronautical and astronautical engineering from the University of Kansas, and a master's in management from the Massachusetts Institute of Technology as an Alfred P. Sloan Research Fellow.

Berrett–Koehler
Publishers

Berrett-Koehler is an independent publisher dedicated to an ambitious mission: *Connecting people and ideas to create a world that works for all.*

Our publications span many formats, including print, digital, audio, and video. We also offer online resources, training, and gatherings. And we will continue expanding our products and services to advance our mission.

We believe that the solutions to the world's problems will come from all of us, working at all levels: in our society, in our organizations, and in our own lives. Our publications and resources offer pathways to creating a more just, equitable, and sustainable society. They help people make their organizations more humane, democratic, diverse, and effective (and we don't think there's any contradiction there). And they guide people in creating positive change in their own lives and aligning their personal practices with their aspirations for a better world.

And we strive to practice what we preach through what we call "The BK Way." At the core of this approach is *stewardship,* a deep sense of responsibility to administer the company for the benefit of all of our stakeholder groups, including authors, customers, employees, investors, service providers, sales partners, and the communities and environment around us. Everything we do is built around stewardship and our other core values of *quality, partnership, inclusion,* and *sustainability.*

This is why Berrett-Koehler is the first book publishing company to be both a B Corporation (a rigorous certification) and a benefit corporation (a for-profit legal status), which together require us to adhere to the highest standards for corporate, social, and environmental performance. And it is why we have instituted many pioneering practices (which you can learn about at www.bkconnection.com), including the Berrett-Koehler Constitution, the Bill of Rights and Responsibilities for BK Authors, and our unique Author Days.

We are grateful to our readers, authors, and other friends who are supporting our mission. We ask you to share with us examples of how BK publications and resources are making a difference in your lives, organizations, and communities at www.bkconnection.com/impact.

Dear reader,

Thank you for picking up this book and welcome to the worldwide BK community! You're joining a special group of people who have come together to create positive change in their lives, organizations, and communities.

What's BK all about?

Our mission is to connect people and ideas to create a world that works for all.

Why? Our communities, organizations, and lives get bogged down by old paradigms of self-interest, exclusion, hierarchy, and privilege. But we believe that can change. That's why we seek the leading experts on these challenges—and share their actionable ideas with you.

A welcome gift

To help you get started, we'd like to offer you a **free copy** of one of our bestselling ebooks:

www.bkconnection.com/welcome

When you claim your **free ebook**, you'll also be subscribed to our blog.

Our freshest insights

Access the best new tools and ideas for leaders at all levels on our blog at ideas.bkconnection.com.

Sincerely,

Your friends at Berrett-Koehler